Gender
and
Sexuality

In Light of Esoteric Science

RON MACFARLANE

Published 2017 by
Greater Mysteries Publications
Mission, BC, Canada

Cover Design: Ron MacFarlane

Printed in the United States of America

ISBN:
ISBN-13: 978-0994007773
ISBN-10: 0994007779

DEDICATION

This work is reverentially dedicated
to the Heavenly Father and the Holy Mother,
the complementary divine persons of the Trinitarian God,
who are the ultimate sources
of the masculine and feminine genderization
that permeates and pervades the entire created universe
from atoms to angels

CONTENTS

GENDER
AND
SEXUALITY

INTRODUCTION

SINCE THE DAWN of mankind, human beings have unquestioningly accepted the self-evident biological truth that there are only two distinct sexes—male and female. Furthermore, this truth was understood to be divinely established, as indicated in the ancient Hebrew writings of Moses: "So God created man in his own image ... male and female he created them. And God blessed them" (Gen 1:27, 28).

Similarly with the concomitant truth that there are only two distinct genders—masculine and feminine. Moreover, in ancient times the dual genders were seen as fundamental and complementary universal principles that infused and fashioned everything in the created cosmos. One familiar expression of this ancient metaphysical belief is the Chinese Taoist principles of yin and yang.

Throughout history, stable and productive family units, tribal groupings, social communities, and even vast empires were globally established on the exigent foundational truths of sexuality and gender—that is—until very recently.

Beginning in the mid-1950s, what had been perennially and universally accepted regarding sex and gender began to be academically questioned and challenged. This ideological heterodoxy quickly accelerated in the 1960s with the inception and radical cultural impact of the sexual revolution and the feminist movement. Increased and well-organized gay and lesbian activism in the 1970s also did much to publicly reject the traditional dichotomies of male–female and masculine–feminine in order to promote a novel range of non-normative sexualities and exotic gender categories.

By the early 2000s, sociological theorists, academic institutions, media organizations, civil rights groups, medical associations, political parties, national governments and international agencies were all becoming involved in a cultural drive to "mainstream" this radically-new and socially-transformative gender ideology.

But to a large percentage of today's citizens throughout Western society, this cultural revolution of gender ideology has been unexpectedly and uninvitedly infiltrating their established lives and communities with a discordant cacophony of bizarre sexual and gender ideas, terms and expressions; such as: gender identity, gender expression, gender roles, gender socialization, gender fluidity, gender ambiguity (ambigender), third gender (trigender), non-binary gender, non-gender, gender neutral, agender, gender dysphoria, gender perspective, genderqueer, biological gender, hormonal gender, gonadic gender, cisgender, pangender, transgender, sexual orientation, bisexual, transsexual, intersexual, omnisexual, asexual, androgynous and two-spirit.

While even to casual observation, it is evident that this contemporary sexual revolution is causing fierce political and social upheaval, what can be perplexing to a deeper spiritual analysis are questions such as: "What exactly are sexuality and gender; and are they synonymous or different? What is causing the current sexual revolution? Why is it occurring at this particular time in world history? Is this sexual revolution progressive or regressive; beneficial or harmful? Are there spiritual forces and beings involved in this upheaval; and are they godly or evil?"

Though these questions can certainly be spiritually addressed by traditional Western theology, a much deeper, meaningful, lasting and comprehensive understanding can only be provided by the superphysical research and hidden wisdom of esoteric science.[1]

This particular discourse, then—*Gender and Sexuality in Light of Esoteric Science*—heavily relies on ancient Yogic teachings, age-old Egyptian Hermetic philosophy, hidden Rosicrucian wisdom and the anthroposophical research of clairvoyant investigator, Rudolf Steiner (1861–1925) to profoundly and penetratingly address these important questions.

Esoteric science will convincingly explain why there are, in reality, only two sexes—male and female; and only two genders—masculine and feminine. Anything else is an unreal and delusional abstraction, hypothesis or conjecture.

In order to rationally embrace the binary truth of gender—masculine and feminine—it will be necessary to first understand the Trinitarian nature of God, and then perceive how the divine nature is faithfully reflected throughout the created universe, including human existence. After which, in order to similarly embrace the binary truth of human sexuality—male and female—it will be necessary to clairvoyantly trace the history and development of mankind on earth, back to far-distant primordial ages.

It will be shown that throughout human existence on earth, powerful supernatural beings and forces—both beneficial and inimical—have been intimately and significantly involved in the evolution and development of human sexuality. Moreover, despite the appalling lack of contemporary human awareness, this supernatural involvement has continued into the present day.

The much-celebrated "freedoms" brought about by the sexual revolution will be seen and understood to be an inimical supernatural assault on reason, reality, nature and progressive human evolution, particularly by Luciferic and Ahrimanic beings and forces.[2] The current state of sexual and gender confusion, therefore, is not regarded as a positive development by esoteric science; but rather a seriously-harmful and seductive delusionary entrapment that must be challenged, arrested and positively corrected.

CHAPTER 1

AN ESOTERIC HISTORICAL BACKGROUND TO UNIVERSAL GENDER

1.1 The Etymology and Original Meaning of "Gender"

UNFORTUNATELY TODAY, the original meaning and profound significance of the word "gender"—denoting masculine and feminine—has been lost to ordinary understanding. Even the academic gender theorists themselves disagree as to the meaning: some use gender synonymously and interchangeably with sex (male–female); some maintain a distinction between gender and sex, but postulate that gender is simply a relative social construct; while some assert that gender only applies to grammatical usage in language.

The modern English word "gender" can be traced back to the Latin "genus" meaning "kind," "type" or "sort." It is also more meaningfully related to the Greek root "gen-" which means "to produce"; appearing in such words as "engender," "generate" and "genesis." The Greek root provides a far better indication of the ancient spiritual meaning of gender;

that in order to produce, actuate, create, propagate, procreate, originate or effectuate anything in the universe, the dual principles of masculinity and femininity are fundamentally necessary.

An echo of this primal understanding of cosmic gender is still retained in Chinese Taoist philosophy as the familiar concept of yin-yang; where yin is regarded as the universal feminine principle, and yang is regarded as the universal masculine principle. Both principles are seen as complementary and indispensible in effecting all life and activity throughout Nature. As expressed by the ancient Chinese philosopher, Lao-tzu (604 BC–501 BC) in the *Tao Te Ching*:

> Tao engenders One;
> One engenders Two;
> Two engenders Three;
> Three engenders all things.
> All things carry the yin (femininity)
> while embracing the yang (masculinity).
> Neutralizing energy brings them into harmony.

The equally-legendary Chinese philosopher, Confucius (551 BC–479 BC) similarly stated:

> Yin and yang, male and female, strong and weak, rigid and tender, heaven and earth, light and darkness, thunder and lightning, cold and warmth, good and evil ... the interplay of opposite principles constitutes the universe.

1.2   The Ancient Hermetic Principle of Gender

The closely-guarded esoteric teachings commonly known as "Hermeticism"—since they are believed to have been founded by the mysterious Egyptian initiate, Hermes Trismegistus, the so-called "scribe of the gods"—have also extolled the spiritual truth that the bipolar principle of gender (masculinity and femininity) underpins the entire universe, and is not simply a human characteristic. As stated in *The Kybalion* (Three Initiates; 1940):

> [I]n the light of the Hermetic Teachings, you will be able to see that the energizing of the Feminine Principle by the Vibratory Energy of the Masculine Principle is in accordance to the universal laws of nature, and that the natural world affords countless analogies whereby the principles may be understood. In fact, the Hermetic Teachings show that the very creation of the Universe follows the same law, and that in all creative manifestation, upon the planes of the spiritual, the mental, and the physical, there is always in operation this principle of Gender—this manifestation of the Masculine and the Feminine Principles.

1.3 Universal Gender According to Rosicrucian Teaching

The ancient spiritual understanding that masculine and feminine gender are two complementary principles of Nature that pervade the entire universe, and which are essential in the propagation of all life and activity has also been secretly guarded by the Rosicrucian Brotherhood since medieval times.

Even though the public dissemination of Rosicrucian mystery teaching has been historically rare, one such rudimentary release is *The Secret Doctrine of the Rosicrucians* by Magus Incognito (1949). Concerning universal gender, this rather illuminating volume has stated the following:

> According to the Secret Doctrine of the Rosicrucians, there are present in All Creation the activities of a Male

Principle and a Female Principle, both Universal in Nature, Character and Extent—both Opposing Aspects of the World Soul—which act and react, one upon the other, and thus produce all Creative Activity and the "Cosmic Becoming" or Universal Activity and Change.

1.4 Characteristics of Universal Gender According to Yin-Yang Philosophy

Even though the ancient Chinese concept of yin and yang can be very helpful in understanding the dual universal principles of masculine and feminine gender, there has also been some unfortunate associated misunderstandings over the centuries.

In the area of helpful understanding, contemporary esoteric science fully agrees with yin-yang philosophy that the universal feminine principle (yin) and the universal masculine principle (yang) may *appear* to be diametrically-opposing polarities; but in reality they are harmoniously-complementary and mutually-symbiotic principles. Moreover, these twin gender principles always co-exist together; they are never apart in Nature. There is never the masculine principle in operation (in whatever form or manifestation) without the corresponding activity of the feminine principle; and vice versa. Consequently, both gender principles are equally and fundamentally necessary throughout the cosmos; one is not more important or essential than the other (see Figure 1 on page 6).

The unfortunate misunderstandings that have historically occurred are due primarily to certain characteristics that have been commonly associated with the yin and yang principles. For example, the feminine yin principle has been commonly characterized as "negative, passive and dark"; while the masculine yang principle has been commonly characterized as "positive, active and light." While on one level universal phenomena can certainly be understood as the mutual interaction of positive and negative, active and passive, light and dark, there is a deeper more esoteric understanding of these particular characteristics that better illustrate the masculine and feminine principles in Nature.

Take, to begin with, the dichotomy of "positive and negative." "Negative" is most commonly understood to be an adverse, nullifying activity or condition; not one of effusive generation and expansion. And yet, in the case of a galvanic (voltaic) cell, it is the negative pole (or anode) that actively generates the profusion of electron particles which result in an electric current. In this particular positive and negative duality, the negative pole is hardly an adverse, nullifying condition. Likewise with the universal feminine principle (yin), the characteristic of negativity also needs to be properly associated with growth, generation and expansion.

Similarly with the yin-yang dichotomy of "passive and active." "Passive" is most commonly understood to be static inertia and motionless receptivity. But in the case of human reproduction, once the passive and relatively-motionless female ovum has "received" the motile male spermatozoon, then a process of rapid cellular growth and expansion is generated. Likewise with the universal feminine principle (yin), the characteristic of passive receptivity is the necessary pre-condition for growth, generation and expansion to occur in Nature.

Thirdly, considering the yin-yang dichotomy of "light and dark," "darkness" is very often regarded as a desolate and empty void of nothingness; when in fact, it is far better understood as a still-condition of latent potentiality. Darkness as a characteristic of the universal feminine principle (yin), therefore, should not be regarded as an emptiness; but rather as a dormant condition of latent possibilities, waiting to be stirred into life. This notion has been wonderfully described in the biblical book of Genesis, where the spirit of God stirred the darkness that was upon the face of the cosmogonic deep; thereby bringing forth the heavens and the earth.

From the forgoing analysis of yin-yang philosophy, it should be readily apparent how important it is to have a deeper and clearer understanding of the familiar characteristics attributed to universal gender. Students of history will no doubt have observed that superficial interpretations of the universal gender dichotomies of positive-negative, active-passive and light-dark have been used to subjugate and repress women in many Eastern cultures. Historically attributing the erroneously-understood, universal feminine (yin) characteristics of "negative, passive and dark" to actual women in society, has unfortunately provided a philosophical rationale for male domination in many Eastern cultures.

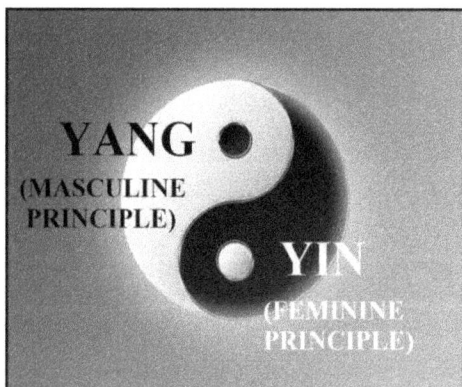

Figure 1: Chinese Taijitu Symbol of Yin and Yang

1.5 Characteristics of Universal Gender According to Esoteric Science

In yin-yang philosophy, many of the polarized characteristics attributed to the masculine and feminine genders do not actually describe the essential activity of the two universal principles, but rather their possible effects or manifestations. For example, the universal feminine principle (yin) is often characterized as "wet, cold, night, winter and moon"; and the universal masculine principle (yang) is often characterized as "dry, warm, day, summer and sun." A much deeper and more meaningful understanding has been carefully guarded throughout the centuries within the esoteric teachings of Hermeticism and Rosicrucianism.

According to esoteric science, the universal masculine principle—on every plane and level of existence—is characterized by a compulsion to contract inwardly towards a central point. This centralizing contraction results in an increasing concentration and densification to an intense point of critical mass. At this nadir of centralization, after a still moment of constrained singularity, a super-charged excitation occurs.

Conversely, the universal feminine principle—on every plane and level of existence—is characterized by a compulsion to expand outwardly towards a surrounding periphery. This decentralizing expansion results in an increasing proliferation and diffusion to a radiated circumference of critical rarefaction. At this zenith of multiplicity, after a still moment of enervated distension, a super-attenuated subsidence occurs.

It is also important to esoterically understand that the universal masculine and feminine principles are not lifeless, mechanical forces in Nature; but are instead living operations that are fundamentally essential in generating the forms, manifestations and activities of cosmic life.

Viewed, then, as vital generative principles, the universal masculine gender is also understood to be the "initiating" or "fertilizing" principle in Nature. The masculine impulsion towards a concentrated, centralized point provides the "seed" impulse for universal generation; while the feminine impulse towards an expanded periphery causes the seed impulse to grow and multiply. Once again, it is readily apparent that both gender principles are vitally necessary for every and all procreative activities in Nature.

Likewise expressed in Hermetic philosophy:

> The part of the Masculine principle seems to be that of directing a certain inherent energy toward the Feminine principle, and thus starting into activity the creative processes. But the Feminine principle is the one always doing the active creative work—and this is so on all planes. And yet, each principle is incapable of operative energy without the assistance of the other. In some forms of life, the two principles are combined in one organism. For that matter, everything in the organic world manifests both genders—there is always the Masculine present in the Feminine form, and the Feminine present in the Masculine form. (*The Kybalion*; 1940)

1.6 Big Bang Creation as a Macrocosmic Manifestation of Universal Gender

Since the universal masculine principle and the universal feminine principle are in constant operation throughout Nature, they're equally responsible for super-galactic, macrocosmic forms and events; as well as for infinitesimally-small, microcosmic forms and events. Even the creation and expansion of the entire universe itself is an awe-inspiring testament to the ubiquitous operations of the twin universal genders.

Modern science recognizes that the universe began as an infinitely small, infinitely hot and infinitely dense gravitational point called a "singularity." For unclear reasons, about 13.82

billion years ago, the cosmic singularity began to rapidly expand outwardly (the "Big Bang")[3] like a macrocosmic balloon, thereby generating physical space and time. Immediately after the Big Bang, a profusion of subatomic particles, gas clouds, globular clusters, stars and galaxies began to form.

While empirical science has a reasonable hypothesis of *how* the universe began, it fails to explain *why* the universe began as a singularity, *why* did the Big Bang occur, *why* such a proliferation of subatomic particles and astronomical formations soon after the Big Bang, and *why* does the universe (as a whole) continue to expand outwardly?

According to esoteric science, the answer is straightforward and concise—the universe was, and is, simply conforming to the principles of universal gender. The infinitely compressed cosmic singularity was the result of the centralizing, contracting activity of the universal masculine principle, which also provided the initiating "spark"—the cosmic seed-impulse—for universal expansion.

Once the masculine Big Bang ignition had occurred, the universal feminine principle was stimulated into generative activity and rapidly began a cosmic process of atomic, stellar and galactic formation, as well as intense outward expansion—thereby generating physical space and time. Since the universe is continuing to expand, it obviously remains under the direction of the universal feminine principle. Common language is therefore wisely intuitive in referring to our present expanding and proliferating universe as "Mother Nature."

1.7 Subatomic Particles as a Microcosmic Manifestation of Universal Gender

The characteristic operation and application of the

universal masculine and universal feminine principles can also be supersensibly observed at the subatomic level of the cosmos as well. From an esoteric-science perspective, the profusion of exotic subatomic particles (for all their uniqueness and variety) share a single, fundamental genesis—they are all infinitesimal vortices of movement (energy) in the cosmic ether.

Even though empirical science in the late-nineteenth century briefly postulated the existence of a "luminiferous or light ether" as the rarefied and invisible medium for light-wave propagation, it has since dropped the term in favour of the less-mystical designations: "Einsteinian space," "physical space" or simply "space."[4]

In contemporary scientific parlance, then, electromagnetic waves (such as light) and subatomic particles (such as photons) travel through "space." In spite of some agreement with physical science, esoteric science still prefers to use the older term "ether," rather than "space," since there are some significant differences between the two. For example, according to anthroposophical research, there are four important gradations of ether: (1) warmth ether, (2) light ether, (3) tone (or chemical) ether and (4) life ether. Empirical science does not similarly recognize four gradations of "space."

What to empirical science is a subatomic particle mechanically spinning in space is regarded by esoteric science as an infinitesimal vortex of energy rapidly rotating according to the principles of universal gender in one of the four ethers. As with every instance of cosmic formation (large and small), the generation of subatomic particles begins with an application of the universal masculine principle.

An infinitesimal contraction towards a centralized point begins in the etheric medium. The combination of centripetal contraction together with the outward motion of the expanding universe causes an immediate angular momentum to occur. In other words, when the ether contracts inwardly, it does so with a spiraling motion that causes the etheric medium to spin around the centralized point, like a minute vortex.

As the masculine-induced contraction continues, the spinning vortex inwardly accelerates until it sparks a sudden outward expansion under the direction of the universal feminine principle. The feminine-induced centrifugal expansion rapidly diffuses the etheric medium outwardly in all directions. At a certain outer circumference, the force of centrifugal expansion is exhausted, and the etheric medium begins to once again contract under the direction of the universal masculine principle (see Figure 2 on page 12).

Once a subatomic vortex (particle) has been generated, the rhythmic back-and-forth, in-and-out oscillation between masculine-contraction and feminine-expansion can theoretically continue almost indefinitely since the etheric medium is essentially frictionless. In reality, the surrounding actions of other subatomic vortex-particles and various powerful natural forces will most often shorten their independent life-spans.

The rapid back-and-forth oscillations of spinning subatomic vortex-particles is what has been commonly known by empiricists and esotericists alike as "vibration." Since subatomic particles form the basis of all chemical activity throughout the universe, the entire physical world can be correctly understood to be in a constant state of vibration. In fact, differences in the rapidity of vibration are responsible for the various perceptible states of physical matter: solid matter vibrates slower than liquid matter; and gaseous matter vibrates faster than liquid matter.

The vibratory oscillations of subatomic particles—singly and in combination—also generate wave movement in the etheric medium. Differences in the rapidity (or frequency) of these etheric waves account for the differences of various known energies. In the case of electromagnetic energy, radio waves vibrate slower than microwaves; and ultraviolet waves vibrate faster than visible light waves.

Also worth mentioning in connection with the operation of the universal gender principles at the subatomic level, the masculine centripetal contraction toward a centralized point in the ether is what is commonly known as "gravity." Moreover, the centralized compressive and contractive force of masculine gravity causes a densification of the etheric medium which is commonly referred to as "mass." This simply and concisely explains why the nucleus of a subatomic particle— and likewise an atom—has far greater mass than the rarified feminine perimeter.

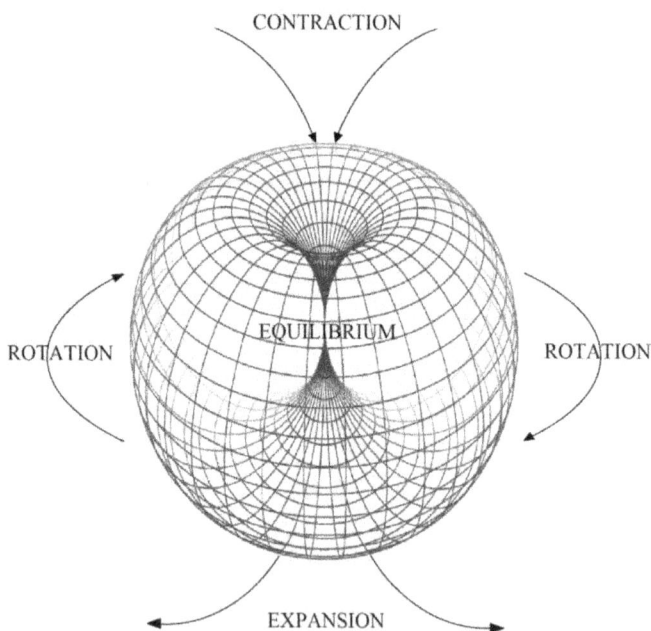

Figure 2: Simplified Example of Generic Subatomic Particle

1.8 Thought Formation as a Mental Manifestation of Universal Gender

Since the universal gender principles fundamentally operate on all planes and levels of the cosmos, their activity can also be observed on the mental plane. To esoteric science, mental activity is not generated by human brain tissue, nor is it confined to the interior of the human skull. "Mind-stuff" is understood to be an ultra-rarified medium that transcends matter and energy, and which pervades the entire universe. The human brain is simply a complex anatomical organ designed to temporarily appropriate and employ small quanta of universal mind stuff for individual use. Human thinking, then, is one such employment.

Unlike the creation of the Big Bang universe and the generation of subatomic particles, human beings are consciously involved in the process of thinking, and thereby themselves utilize the principles of universal gender. Most thinkers are, unfortunately, unaware of the supersensible nature of human mentation; and therefore act much more instinctively than knowingly.

Aside from memory formation and recall, thinking will characteristically involve the generation and utilization of original ideas. While pure, brain-free mental activity is faster than the speed of light, when thought is processed by the physical brain it is stepped-down to the speed of electro-chemical conduction. Viewed clairvoyantly, a typical thought in many respects resembles a generic subatomic particle. Both are vortices whirling in space—though a subatomic particle is spinning in physical space, while a thought is spinning in mental space. As described in Yoga philosophy:

> In the first place the word "Mind" is used as synonymous with *Chitta*, or Mind-substance, which is the Universal Mind Principle. From this *Chitta*, Mind-substance, or Mind, all the material of the millions of personal minds is

obtained.

Mind-substance in Sanskrit is called *"Chitta,"* and a wave in the *Chitta* (which wave is the combination of Mind and Energy) is called *"Vritta,"* which is akin to what we call a "thought." In other words it is "mind in action," whereas *Chitta* is "mind in repose." *Vritta*, when literally translated means "a whirlpool or eddy in the mind," which is exactly what a thought really is. (Yogi Ramacharaka; *A Series of Lessons in Raja Yoga*; 1934)

As opposed to thoughts that simply rise up into awareness from the subconscious levels of the mind, the conscious generation of a thought begins with an effort of mental concentration. What most contemporary thinkers don't realize is that the performance of mental concentration is an application of the universal masculine principle; and as such will contract mental space-substance to a centralized point.

In doing so, the mind-stuff is increasingly compressed and densified. On the physical plane, when matter is compressed it heats up; similarly on the mental plane—when mind-stuff is compressed it begins to generate a degree of "mental warmth." If mental concentration is held long enough, the steadily-increasing pressure and heat formation will cause the mind-stuff to ignite with a sudden burst of mental illumination.

This burst of mental illumination is commonly experienced as an "ah-ha moment"—a moment of mental realization and insight. Artists have fancifully conveyed this mental light-burst by drawing a light bulb above a person's head. Moreover, this mental spark of illumination is what is commonly known as an "idea."

On the mental plane, an idea acts as the universal masculine seed-impulse that stimulates the universal feminine principle into generating a variety of mental configurations and formulations, commonly known as "thoughts."

1.9 What is the Role and Function of the Universal Gender Principles?

Even though the universal gender principles operate exactly the same on all planes of existence, the substances employed and the effects that are produced can be quite different. Qualitatively, a mental thought is much different than a subatomic particle, even though both are generated by the interaction of the two universal gender principles.

In other words, the two gender principles—the universal masculine and the universal feminine—are together required to generate the astonishing wealth, variety and richness of life throughout the cosmos. Even the very existence of the cosmos itself is dependent on these two gender principles.

Absolutely nothing in the universe, then, is conceived, created, generated, originated, produced, engendered, propagated or comes into existence without the mutual interaction of the universal masculine principle and the universal feminine principle. Esoterically understood, then, there are two and only two gender principles—masculine and feminine—that creatively operate throughout the universe. Any talk of a "third gender" or an exotic variety of genders is simply idle conjecture that has no connection to reality.

It will be quite obvious at this point, therefore, that the function of universal gender—the essential role of the masculine principle and the feminine principle—is to bring forth abundant creations, creatures, life-forms and sentient beings throughout the cosmos.

CHAPTER 2

THE DIVINE ORIGIN OF UNIVERSAL GENDER

2.1 Self-Awareness and Universal Gender

THE DEFINING CHARACTERISTIC of human beings (as opposed to minerals, plants and animals) is self-awareness (or ego-consciousness). To be sure, animals are aware of their surroundings and bodily processes; but individual animals are not conscious of being a separate ego-self—"they are aware; but not aware of being aware." Consequently, at this stage in earthly-evolution, ordinary members of the animal kingdom are incapable of conceptualizing, "I am."

This concise but little understood declaration of self-awareness—"I am"—is a remarkable and powerful mental abstraction or "word-logo"; comprised of two unique words: "I" and "am." "I" (in English) is the word-symbol for self-identity or ego-being; and "am" is the word-symbol for conscious-knowing or cognizant-awareness. "I am," then, is a succinct way of conceptualizing and expressing that "I am aware that I exist."

Self-awareness, then, as indicated by the word-logo, "I am," is a combination of two essential intrapsychic elements: (1) ego-being (or self), and (2) knowing (or consciousness). Even though the process is largely instinctive for most people, in order to consciously comprehend our state of being—our "I"— it is necessary to mentally concentrate and focus on a single point in the head between and slightly behind the eyes. It should be obvious, then, that the human experience of our ego-self or I-being results from an intrapsychic application of the universal masculine principle.

Contrastingly, in order to actively comprehend our state of conscious-knowing, it is necessary to mentally expand and distend our attention outwardly, beyond the confines of the head, to a far-distant periphery in space. It should be equally obvious, then, that the human experience of our conscious-knowing or cognizant-awareness results from an intrapsychic application of the universal feminine principle.

Human self-awareness, then, is a consequent effect of the interaction between the universal masculine and the universal feminine principles; without which there would be no "I am" experience.

2.2 Human Personhood as a Reflection of Divine Personhood

Self-awareness and the consequent ability to meaningfully declare, "I am," is the basic requirement of "personhood"; of existing as a "person," and not as a "creature" or as a "thing." Sadly, due primarily to present-day materialistic science and secular-atheistic enculturation, many individuals living today do not realize or appreciate that human personhood has a divine, supernatural origin.[5]

Esoteric science basically concurs with empirical science that to sensory perception the physical world of matter and energy appears to be lifeless, insensate, amoral and purposeless. Chemical activity throughout the universe does not exhibit signs of life, consciousness, morality or self-directed purpose and intent. Hydrogen atoms do not consciously worry about whether it is right or wrong to combine with oxygen atoms; nor do they purposefully combine because they themselves intend to form water.

The thorny existential dilemma, however, is that within this vast universal ocean of lifeless, insensate, amoral and purposeless chemical activity exist living, conscious, thoughtful, sentient human beings who purposefully and morally direct their actions and behaviour. The only obvious and logical explanation to this cosmic paradox is—if life, consciousness, morality and purpose are not generated by the natural world, then they *must* have a supernatural origin instead.

Transcendently analogous to the origin of the universe where all matter and energy derives from one solitary source—the Big Bang singularity—all self-aware beings existing within the cosmos (whether human, angelic or seraphic)[6] are derived from a single supernatural source—the one supreme being of God. God is the supernatural source of all life, consciousness, morality and purpose.

The supreme personhood of God, then, is the ultimate source and perfect archetype for all degrees of personhood existing within the created universe. As such, the supreme personhood of God transcendently exhibits the three absolute essentials of personhood: (1) ego-being (or self), (2) knowing (or consciousness) and (3) self-awareness. In the case of God, however, these three absolute essentials are raised to an infinite degree of perfection, existing as: (1) omnipotent total-being, (2) omniscient all-consciousness and (3) supernal self-awareness (see Figure 3 on page 20).

SUPERNAL
SELF-AWARENESS

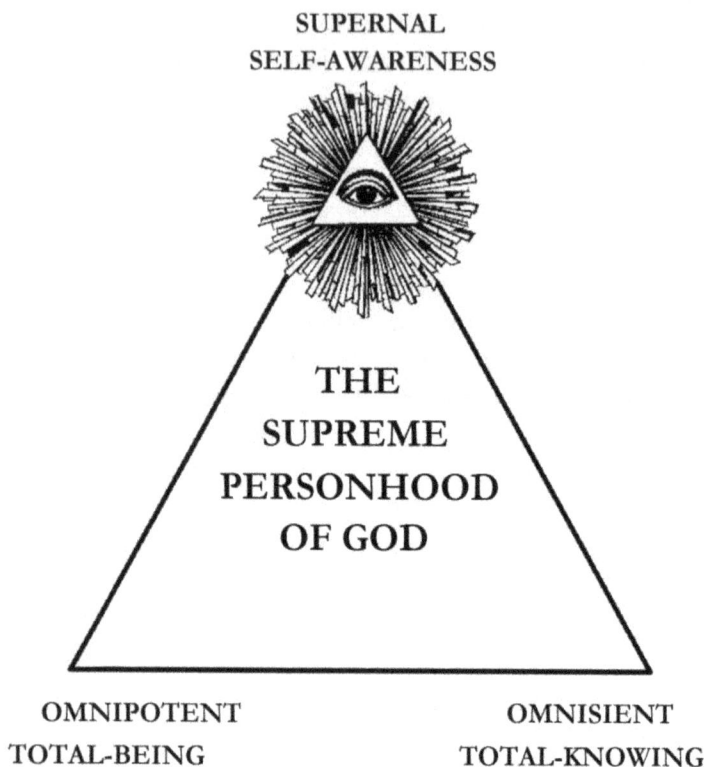

THE
SUPREME
PERSONHOOD
OF GOD

OMNIPOTENT
TOTAL-BEING

OMNISIENT
TOTAL-KNOWING

Figure 3: The Supreme Personhood of God

2.3 The Personhood of God and Divine Gender

Supernally analogous to the human experience of self (or ego-being), the supreme-being of God is the single centralized-point of absolute contraction of the divine nature (commonly known as "spirit"). This centralizing contraction is induced by the divine will, and corresponds to the operation of the universal masculine principle within the created cosmos. In truth, the divine centralizing contraction of spirit to the point of omnipotent total-being is the archetypal source of the universal masculine principle. The universal masculine principle is, then, an imperfect and limited reflection of the omnipotent centralizing activity within the spirit-nature of God.

Furthermore, supernally analogous to the human experience of knowing (or consciousness), the all-consciousness of God is the infinite expansion of the divine spirit-nature. This wisdom-filled, all-embracive expansion corresponds to the operation of the universal feminine principle within the created cosmos. Once again in truth, the divine procreative expansion of spirit to the extended degree of omniscient all-knowing is the archetypal source of the universal feminine principle. The universal feminine principle is, then, an imperfect and limited reflection of the omniscient, expansive activity within the spirit-nature of God.

Divine self-awareness, then, is the union of divine being and divine knowing; or to rephrase this more comprehensively: the rhythmic interaction of the divine-masculine contractive-activity of supreme being and the divine-feminine expansive-activity of total knowing generates supernal self-awareness. Logically, since God is eternal, the super-vibratory motion of spirit which generates supernal self-awareness has had no beginning, nor will it have an end.

Human self-awareness is best understood as a limited and imperfect reflection of divine self-awareness. In very truth, without the pre-existence of divine self-awareness, there would be no human self-awareness.

2.4 Divine Gender as Living Personifications of God's Nature

Unlike the astounding array of finite and temporal life-forms existing throughout the known universe, the spirit-nature of God is infinite and eternal. As such, compared to all created beings the living God is not just real—but "hyper-real"—to a degree entirely incomprehensible to finite minds with limited consciousness. Therefore, every feature, characteristic, attribute or distinction of God's spirit-nature is imbued with super-elevated life and reality. This is particularly so with the three fundamental essentials of divine personhood—they are so imbued with deific life and reality that they exist as distinct divine personifications.

The omnipotent total-being of God's spirit-nature exists as the "divine masculine personification," also known esoterically as the "Heavenly Father." The omniscient all-consciousness of God's spirit-nature exists as the "divine feminine personification," also known esoterically as the "Holy Mother." Since the supernal self-awareness of God's spirit-nature is the perfect union of the Heavenly Father and the Holy Mother, this third divine-essential is esoterically known as the "Eternal Son"[7] (see Figure 4 below).

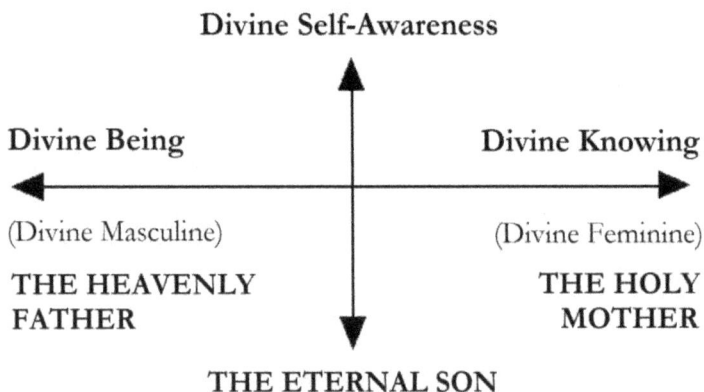

Figure 4: The Three Divine Personifications

2.5 Divine Gender and the Trinitarian Nature of God's Existence

From what has been discussed thus far, it is obvious that esoteric science fully agrees with traditional Western theology that the One God is a perfect unity of three deific personifications—or simply, "three divine persons." Furthermore, this "Trinity" of divine persons is agreed to be co-existent, co-equal and consubstantial with one another.

There is, however, a couple of noticeable differences. In Western theology, the divine Trinity is understood to be Father, Son and Holy Spirit; whereas the esoteric understanding of the divine Trinity is Father, Son and Holy Mother.[8]

Moreover, in Western theology it is believed that the divine person of the Father eternally generates (or "begets") the divine person of the Son; and together, the Father and the Son eternally generate (or "spirate") the Holy Spirit.[9] The esoteric understanding, however, is that the divine person of the Father together with the divine person of the Holy Mother eternally generate the divine person of the Son.

Esoterically speaking, then, the divine person of the Son is not a third gender; but rather the perfect union of the only two genders in real (divine) existence—the Heavenly Father (divine masculinity) and the Holy Mother (divine femininity).

Given the real-existence and complementarity of the Heavenly Father and the Holy Mother, it's abundantly obvious that divine gender is transcendently more alive, personal and powerful than the various cosmic manifestations of universal gender. The infinite and eternal rhythmic interplay between the divine masculine (Heavenly Father) and the divine feminine (Holy Mother) is superlatively beyond any mechanical-style, vibratory oscillations that generate subatomic particles. As well, divine gender is transcendently superior to any back-and-forth mental vacillations which generate human thoughts and ideas. Divine gender is even infinitely grander than the recurring collapse and expansion of the entire universe.

The two divine genders, then, are much, much more than simply being universal forces of Nature; or universal mental operations in Nature; or universal principles (laws) of Nature. The two divine genders transcend the entire natural world; but are likewise much more than being simply supernatural forces, supernatural operations or supernatural principles (laws). The two divine genders are fully-alive, deific personifications—divine persons—who have eternally existed in perfect, mutual complementarity.

2.6 Divine Gender as a Relationship of Spiritual Love

Esoteric science and Western theology also mutually accept the revelatory truth that "God is love."[10] How this is esoterically understood is that the spirit-nature of God is synonymous with divine love; that is, divine love *is* the spirit-nature of God. In this light, the two gender distinctions of God's spirit-nature are also correctly understood to be two distinctions of divine love. The Heavenly Father, then, is the perfect personification of divine "masculine" love; and the Holy Mother is the perfect personification of divine "feminine" love.

The eternal, back-and-forth contraction and expansion of God's spirit-nature, then, is best understood as an eternal interchange and infinite reciprocation of divine love between the Heavenly Father and the Holy Mother. Moreover, the Eternal Son is best understood as the perfect union of divine masculine and divine feminine love. As the divine offspring, the Eternal Son is eternally generated by the mutual love of the Heavenly Father and the Holy Mother (see Figure 5 on page 25).

The divine Trinity, then, is best understood as a transcendent, "familial" love-relationship of divine Father, divine Mother and divine Progeny (Son). Of course when applying human familial terms and interactions to God's Trinitarian spirit-nature, it must be kept in mind that they are all raised to a degree of infinite and eternal perfection (unlike the finite and temporal limitations of human nature).[11]

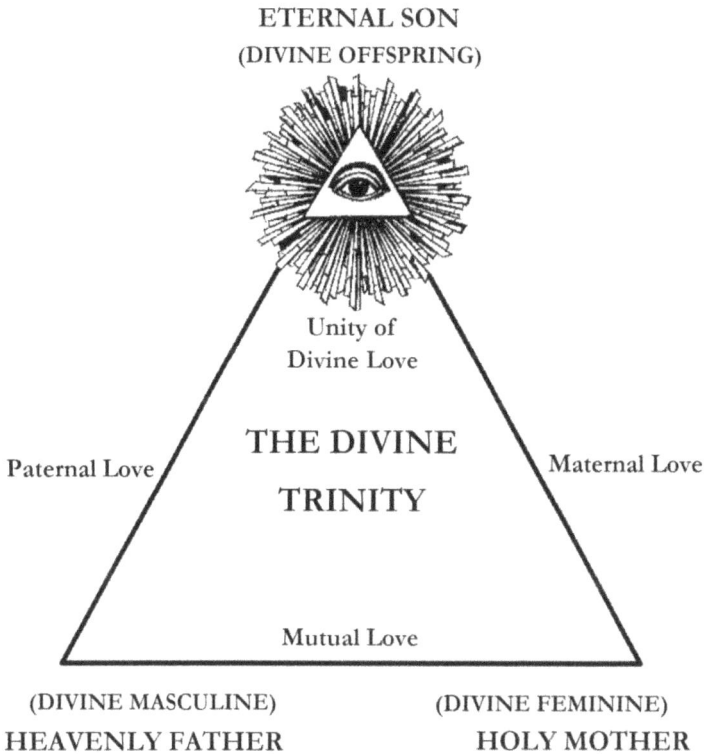

ETERNAL SON
(DIVINE OFFSPRING)

Unity of
Divine Love

THE DIVINE

Paternal Love   Maternal Love

TRINITY

Mutual Love

(DIVINE MASCULINE)   (DIVINE FEMININE)
HEAVENLY FATHER   **HOLY MOTHER**

Figure 5: The Trinity of Divine Love

The co-equal, co-eternal and consubstantial love of the three persons of God is logically the highest and most perfect expression of love in reality. As such, the love of the Trinity serves as the goal and ideal of all love relationships in the created universe. In other words, the principles of universal gender strive to best reflect and manifest the divine gender expressed in Trinitarian love.

Of course the perfect love as expressed in divine gender is transcendently beyond what manifests as human sexuality and procreation. Human sexuality and procreation are temporary, limited, imperfect and undeveloped reflections of divine love as it manifests in the physical world. The remainder of this discourse will thoroughly examine the primordial history and extensive evolutionary development of human sexuality as understood in esoteric science.

CHAPTER 3

AN ESOTERIC BACKGROUND TO UNDERSTANDING HUMAN SEXUALITY

3.1 The Difference Between Gender and Sexuality

UNFORTUNATELY, in present-day academic study and in consequent public conversation, there is a great deal of error and confusion regarding "gender" and "sexuality." Since the ancient understanding of "universal gender" has been lost or ignored, there remains little meaningful distinction between masculine and feminine gender versus male and female sexuality.

Nowadays, instead of asking what "sex" a person is (that is, whether one is male or female), it is becoming increasingly more common to ask what "gender" a person is. Clearly such a "gender" question is not asking whether one is masculine or feminine; but whether one is male or female. In this particular context, then, the word "gender" is used to replace the word "sex"; and is therefore considered to have no separate alternative meaning, other than male and female.[12]

However, in centuries-old esoteric teaching, human

sexuality is regarded as only one particular biological manifestation of universal gender. Worded somewhat differently, male and female sexuality is esoterically understood to be a complex biological manifestation of numerous masculine and feminine forces, processes and operations in Nature. Similarly described in Hermetic philosophy:

> This Principle embodies the truth that there is GENDER manifested in everything—the Masculine and Feminine Principles ever at work. This is true not only of the Physical Plane, but of the Mental and even the Spiritual Planes. On the Physical Plane, this Principle manifests as SEX, on the higher planes it takes higher forms, but the Principle is ever the same. No creation, physical, mental or spiritual, is possible without this Principle ... The Principle of Gender works ever in the direction of generation, regeneration, and creation. (*The Kybalion*; 1940)

Human sexuality, then, esoterically refers to the biological fact of being male or female, not to the underlying formative principles of masculine and feminine gender. Regrettably today, the terms "masculine" and "feminine," having lost their universal status as principles (laws) of Nature, are no longer regarded as the underlying natural determinants of sexuality; but are instead used simply as two adjectives that loosely pertain to the nouns, "male" and "female." In other words, masculine is simply an ambiguous adjective that pertains to the male sex; and feminine is simply an ambiguous adjective that pertains to the female sex.

3.2 What is Human Sexuality?

Esoterically speaking, human sexuality is the unique and

complex manifestation of universal gender as it applies to the procreation and reproduction of human beings. Since individual human beings are esoterically understood to possess multiple interpenetrating vehicles of consciousness and expression, human sexuality encompasses more than just the physical body (see Figure 6 on page 57). Though somewhat less definitive, human sexuality is clairvoyantly seen to also apply to the etheric body. As for the astral body, though there is some noticeable sexual differentiation, it is far less pronounced than that of the physical and etheric bodies. Though the principles of universal gender certainly operate at the soul and spirit levels, sexual differentiation doesn't really apply to the higher planes of existence.

Particularly on the level of the physical and etheric bodies, human beings at the present stage of evolution are separated into two distinct and recognizably-different configurations, referred to in English as the two biological "sexes." One biological sex has been historically termed "male," and the other biological sex has been historically termed "female." While there is some slight sexual differentiation of "maleness" and "femaleness" in the astral body, it is not as sharply defined as the physical and astral bodies. As for the soul and spirit vehicles, a psychic separation into separate male and female configurations does not naturally occur.[13]

From an esoteric standpoint, then, male and female human bodies are indwellingly inhabited by gender-balanced human souls and spirits; that is, by human souls and spirits that have not been bifurcated into separate male and female components.

In accordance with the principle of universal gender, in order for human beings to physically procreate or reproduce, it is absolutely necessary to physically incorporate both masculine and feminine genders. Over long periods of time on earth, the male sex (or "man") has evolved to best incorporate the masculine principle of procreation; and the female sex (or "woman") has evolved to best incorporate the feminine principle of procreation.

3.3 Gender-Induced Features and Characteristics of the Male Sex

Recall that the universal masculine principle is characterized as the contractive, centralizing activity of will-force that provides the fertilizing, initiating seed-impulse of generation and procreation. In the man (or male sex), this gender principle is evidenced in numerous biological systems.

Genetically, male biology is shaped and determined especially by the Y chromosome which contains specific genes that determine male embryonic development, and which are necessary for normal sperm production.

Hormonally, male biology is shaped and determined by the production of androgen, particularly testosterone. Testosterone is crucially necessary to physically embody the masculine attribute of concentrated will-power and strength, that is recognized in broad shoulders and chest; increased muscle mass and strength; taller and larger physical stature; tougher skin; and stronger bone structure.

Genitally, the male reproductive organs (testes, prostate, penis, etc.) embody the masculine principle of formulating and providing the fertilizing seed impulse—in this case, the sperm—for human procreation to occur.[14] The male sperm cell is characteristically condensed, and is one of the smallest cells in the body.

3.4 Gender-Induce Features and Characteristics of the Female Sex

Recall once again that the universal feminine principle is

characterized as the expansive, proliferating activity of wisdom-substance that provides the effusive growth and development necessary for generation and procreation. In the woman (or female sex), this gender principle is also evidenced in numerous biological systems.

Genetically, female biology is shaped and determined especially by the X chromosome, which is much more femininely expansive (about 26 times larger) than the Y chromosome of the male. Conforming to the wisdom-substance attribute of feminine gender, the X chromosome has an excess proportion of genes that are associated with mental functions; specifically, the development of intelligence.

Hormonally, female biology is shaped and determined by the production of estrogen. Estrogen is crucially important to physically prepare the female body to grow, develop, mature and nurture the procreated embryo to the stage of viable, independent existence in accordance with the universal feminine principle. Child-bearing capability is also evident in breast development and in expanded pelvic size.

Genitally, the female reproductive organs (ovaries, Fallopian tubes, uterus, etc.) embody the feminine principle of wise expansion, multiplication and propagation; including the generation of a female sex cell, called an "ova" (from the Latin word "ovum" meaning "egg"). The female ova is one of the largest cells in the body, being about 16 times larger than a sperm cell.

Once again in conformity to the universal feminine principle, the large, spherical female ova remains static and immobile until fertilization by the tiny, pointed, motile male sperm occurs. Whereupon the fertilized ova (now termed a "zygote") begins a process of rapid DNA replication, followed by accelerated cellular division (called "mitosis") to eventually progenerate an entirely new human organism.

3.5 The Purpose of Male and Female Sexuality in Human Beings

Esoteric science fully concurs with mainstream Christianity that since human sexuality ultimately has a divine origin, it also has a divine purpose.[15] Both ideologies reject the pervasive physical-science notion that human life (including human sexuality) is simply a random, accidental chemical occurrence without any underlying purpose or design.

The biological sciences are a solitary exemption, however, since they are reluctantly willing to concede that living organisms (including human beings) have a purpose in life. Unfortunately, the best that Darwinian biology has been able to conceive is the horribly-reductionist notion that the single purpose of all living organisms is "to survive"; or "to propagate their DNA." Human sexuality, then, is simply a means to survive and propagate DNA.

In other words, contemporary physical science is only able to offer two unsatisfactory explanations of human life and sexuality: (1) there is no purpose, and (2) the only purpose is for chemical man-machines to genetically survive. Hypocritically, however, no one—not even staunch atheists, materialists or empirical scientists—honestly live their lives without higher purpose; or consider the arts, philosophy, religion, science, politics, economics, family-life, romantic love and career fulfillment as just meaningless opportunities to spread their DNA.

While it is certainly obvious and readily admitted by esoteric science that the male sex and the female sex are the two fundamental necessities of human reproduction, it is also understood that human sexuality is much more than a chemically-driven biological arrangement to help the human species to survive.[16] From an esoteric point of view, human sexuality generates progressively-new physical and etheric bodies for incarnating souls and spirits. These slowly-refined physical and etheric bodies are necessary for human beings to complete their destined evolutionary development on earth.

Concisely summarized, through the increasing capacity to comprehend and express divine love, human beings are destined to evolve into ethereal, angel-like beings during the Present Earth period of planetary development.[17] The division of humanity into two distinct sexes, male and female, is therefore a crucially-necessary stage in order to achieve this evolutionary goal.

3.6 Human Sexuality Designed to Mirror the Trinitarian Nature of God

Since the life of God is the source and summit of all cosmic existence, every living creature innately and instinctively strives toward divine perfection. Advanced beings who have been endowed with free-will, however, can deliberately resist and oppose this natural yearning for God. Unfortunately, since God is also the ultimate source of joy, happiness, peace and love, by deliberately distancing themselves from their divine Creator, rebellious beings cause themselves loneliness, suffering, unhappiness and sorrow.

In a benevolent effort to assist struggling humanity to begin to learn and experience the joy, happiness, peace and love of God, numerous celestial beings who manifest the divine will have separated undeveloped humanity into two distinct sexes: male and female. By doing so, human souls and spirits have a wonderful opportunity of experiencing—to a humble, finite degree—the infinite and eternal joy of perfect complementarity between the Heavenly Father and the Holy Mother.

As the mutual love between the Heavenly Father and the Holy Mother eternally generates (begets) the Divine Son, so is the sexual love between a man and a women intended to lovingly generate new human life. The human family, therefore, is divinely intended to mirror the Trinitarian love of God. While this high ideal is the ultimate purpose of human sexuality, very often human beings fall well short of transforming sexual love into divine love; and of creating life-giving families that are enduringly nurtured and sustained by divine love.

3.7 Human Sexuality and the Sacrament of Marriage

To assist struggling humanity in establishing stable, enduring and loving family units, benevolent angelic and archangelic overseers originated the marital contract between men and women. Throughout history, this socially-binding agreement took different forms for different cultures. Over time, in many areas of the world, the basic marriage contract between husband and wife became a complicated legal institution of rights and obligations.

Nevertheless, the underlying purpose of marriage has essentially remained the same—by encouraging a strong social and viable bond between men and women, this naturally increases the likelihood of producing healthy, well-adjusted children upon which the continuance of human society is entirely dependent. In short, strong, healthy and productive families ensure a strong, healthy and productive society.

In ancient times, however, the love that was strengthened and encouraged was a consanguineous tribal love; that is, a love between individuals who shared a genealogical blood connection. Familial love, then, was not universal in nature; but instead was typically narrow and exclusionary. It was only with the incarnation of the God-man, Christ-Jesus, that divine love became accessible to human beings on earth.

As biblically depicted with the "marriage at Cana," Christ-

Jesus "blessed" the ritual of marriage by his attendance and his miraculous involvement (changing water into wine). As understood in esoteric science and in Western theology, what is symbolically conveyed with this biblical narrative is the raising of marriage from a contractual "rite," into a powerful "sacrament." As defined by the Catholic Church: "The sacraments are efficacious signs of grace, instituted by Christ and entrusted to the Church, by which divine life is dispensed to us" (paragraph 1131; *Catechism of the Catholic Church*).

In other words, in the new sacrament of marriage, Christ-Jesus himself is spiritually involved in the exchanging of vows between the man and the woman. Moreover, by continuing to supernaturally infuse his own life into the marital life of the conjoined couple, the married man and the married woman are better enabled to transform sexual love into divine love.

In a sacramental marriage, it is intended that the two complementary sexes of man and woman become so united in love for each other that they actually experience a oneness of spirit, similar to the Trinitarian love of God.[18] Not surprisingly, since divine love has only become accessible to human beings since the incarnation of Christ-Jesus two thousand years ago, only a few marital unions are truly imbued with divine love. Moreover, due to an increasingly-atheistic and secular world culture, the divine purpose of marriage is unfortunately being slowly eroded, disregarded and even dismissed.

3.8   The Etheric Body and Human Sexuality

According to the clairvoyant research of esoteric science, the human etheric body also exhibits a two-fold sexual differentiation. This of course is not surprising since the etheric body, as the superphysical vehicle of life-forces, is the shaper, molder, sustainer, repairer and rejuvenator of the physical, chemical body. The etheric body in many respects, then, has a similar but rarified shape and appearance to the physical body.

There is, however, one remarkably significant difference—the etheric body associated with a male physical body is *female*; and the etheric body associated with a female physical body is *male*. Succinctly stated by philosopher and esotericist, Rudolf Steiner (1861–1925) in a lecture given on 18 March 1908 entitled "Man and Woman in Light of Spiritual Science":

> The etheric body is only to a certain extent a picture of the physical body. In regard to the sexes things are different. In the man the etheric body is female and in the woman it is male. However strange it may seem, a deeper observation will disclose the following: Something of the opposite sex lies hidden in each person.

The simple reason for this apparent contradiction is that when the masculine etheric life-forces are deeply and exhaustively incorporated into the physical form in order to transform it into a sexually-male body, only the feminine etheric life-forces remain unincorporated as a supersensible female-envelop surrounding the male physical body.

Conversely, when the feminine etheric life-forces are deeply and exhaustively incorporated into the physical form in order to transform it into a sexually-female body, only the masculine etheric life-forces remain unincorporated as a supersensible male-envelop surrounding the female physical body.

As well as the existence of an *external* complementarity between the male physical body and the female physical body, there also exists an *internal* complementarity between the male physical body and the female etheric body; and between the female physical body and the male etheric body.

Another way of viewing the sexual complementarity

between the physical body and the etheric body is to see in males the *outer* manifestation and expression of concentrated, earthly, masculine forces in the physical body; and the *inner* manifestation and expression of rarified, celestial, feminine forces in the etheric body. Conversely, what can be seen in females is the reverse—the *outer* manifestation and expression of rarified, celestial, feminine forces in the physical body; and the *inner* manifestation and expression of concentrated, earthly, masculine forces in the etheric body.

Here again is evidenced the principle of universal gender which establishes that the masculine and the feminine genders always appear together; there is never the appearance of one gender without the other.

3.9   The Astral Body and Human Sexuality

The human astral body is clairvoyantly observed as a colourfully-scintillating, egg-shaped aura that surrounds and interpenetrates the etheric and physical bodies. It is composed of highly-refined, superphysical substance and forces that are emotional in nature. As such, the astral body is the vehicle of coarse passions, crude feelings, brutish drives, savage impulses, and primitive desires. In short, the astral body is the vehicle for unrefined, instinctual emotions that exist and operate below conscious awareness. The higher, more refined feelings and emotions belong to the soul and spirit vehicles.

Obviously there are strong and powerful feelings, emotions and desires that are unique and different for the male sex and for the female sex. Deep-seated maternal instincts that are typically felt by the female sex aren't necessarily strongly felt by the male sex. Likewise, deep-seated paternal instincts that are typically felt by the male sex aren't necessarily strongly felt by the female sex. Moreover, the emotional experiences of motherhood are naturally different from the emotional experiences of fatherhood. The wide-range of instinctive feelings and emotions that are different for each sex, therefore, has certainly resulted in a sexual polarization within the astral bodies of males and females. Nevertheless, because of the wide range of instinctual feelings and emotions that are also shared by both sexes, the differences aren't great and powerful enough to necessitate separately-constituted astral bodies for males and for females. Male and female human beings, then, share the same astral bodies, but with an emphasis on different sexually-related feelings and emotions.

Noteworthy at this point is to recall that the soul and spirit vehicles of human beings are not significantly different between males and females. While there are certainly masculine and feminine essentials to the soul, they are shared in both males and females. It is incorrect, therefore, to think that there is a female soul or a female spirit that is separate and distinct from a male soul or a male spirit. While the principles of universal gender certainly exist and operate at the soul and spirit levels, it needs to be emphasized that soul and spirit transcend the sexual distinctions of male and female.[19]

3.10   Re-Embodiment and the Alternation of the Sexes

Esoteric science has throughout the ages consistently held to the doctrine of repeated earth-lives, also known as the re-embodiment of souls. It's also important to note, however, that the true esoteric teachings thoroughly reject the horribly-erroneous notion that after death human souls can inhabit animal, plant or mineral forms.

At this stage in evolution, human souls can only re-inhabit human bodies. For this reason, the terms "reincarnation," "transmigration" and "metempsychosis" are deliberately avoided since they very often imply non-human embodiment.

It is obvious, even to casual conversation, that the life experiences of men and women are in many respects unique and profoundly different. For this reason, it is a general rule of human re-embodiment that souls will alternate between male and female. Soul development would certainly become one-sided and unbalanced if every incarnation was one sex or the other. Moreover, the alternation of male and female sexuality with successive re-embodiments is an additional demonstration of the principle of universal gender in action; which principle strives to maintain an equal, balanced and harmonious rhythm between the masculine and feminine genders.

There are, of course, exceptions to this general rule of re-embodiment. Social and cultural conditions at different historical times may determine that a soul is required to repeatedly incarnate as one sex or the other. In prior paternalistic cultures, it may have been necessary to incarnate as a male in order to accomplish significant work as an inventor, politician, artist, explorer, philosopher or religious leader. In this case, clairvoyant research has determined that a maximum of seven incarnations as the same sex is possible before an alternation is strictly required. As described by Rudolf Steiner in a lecture given on 23 June 1907:

> A human being's experiences during an incarnation as a man or as a woman differ so much, that he must incarnate twice during this epoch of 2,200 years, once as a man, and once as a woman, so that two incarnations succeed one another during the average period of one thousand years. Therefore 1,100 to 1,200 years only lie between two incarnations. Generally speaking, it is therefore right that a male and a female incarnation should alternate, but in exceptional cases there may be several succeeding incarnations of the same sex (the

greatest number which could be observed was seven), but then the sex changes. These are exceptions, for as a rule the sexes alternate in the successive incarnations. (From a series of lectures entitled "Theosophy and Rosicrucianism")

CHAPTER 4

THE ESOTERIC HISTORY, DEVELOPMENT
AND FUTURE OF HUMAN SEXUALITY

4.1 The Androgynous Ancestor of Mankind on Earth

NO DOUBT, it will come as a bit of a shock and surprise for some readers to learn that human beings have not always existed in dense chemical bodies; nor have they always been sexually differentiated into male and female. In the distant primordial past of earth evolution, our primitive human ancestors were much more undefined and ethereal in form. In this dreamy, tenuous and animal-like condition, they invisibly wafted about in the dense atmosphere of a molten and magmatic earth.

Furthermore, these vaporous human forms (which resembled jelly-fish, more than any familiar human forms) were sexually "androgynous"; that is, the male and female reproductive life-forces were actively united in a single human form. As such, these dual-sexed human ancestors could reproduce another form without any exterior sexual cooperation (the process was similar to mitosis cell-division, but on a larger scale).

Interestingly, what many mainstream Christians don't realize is that biblical scripture also acknowledges that the "original human" was sexually androgynous. This has been allegorically described in the book of Genesis (2:21–23):

> So the LORD God caused a deep sleep to fall upon the [original] man, and while he slept took one of his ribs and closed up its place with flesh; and the rib which the LORD God had taken from the man he made into a woman and brought her to the man. Then the man said, "This at last is bone of my bones and flesh of my flesh; she shall be called Woman, because she was taken out of Man."

Obviously if woman was taken from the divinely-created original man (allegorically called "Adam": Hebrew for "mankind"), then the original man was both male and female prior to this separation.

4.2 The Separation of the Sexes During the Lemurian Age

Our androgynous human ancestor existed millions and millions of years ago, during an evolutionary period of time known esoterically as the "Lemurian Age." During this extensive period of development (which also spanned millions of years), profound terrestrial and celestial events occurred that dramatically and significantly altered the course of mankind on earth.

By about the middle of the Lemurian Age, the molten earth had cooled sufficiently to form a thin, flexible crust over much of the surface. As the planetary temperature cooled and the surrounding atmospheric solutes condensed, the ethereal human forms correspondingly densified and were gravitationally drawn closer to the surface. The once-diaphanous human form gradually acquired a more gelatinous density, with a more specialized and discernible body-shape, including external appendages for mobility.

Over long periods of time and under the wise direction of advanced celestial beings, the Lemurian human life-form gradually took on a rudimentary animal-like appearance; and dense enough with cartilaginous support to move about the volcanic surface of the earth.

Eventually, the animal-like human forms were refined enough to be gifted with the faint spark of self-conscious awareness from the exalted beings known as "powers" (or "elohim"). At this point, ancestral human "life-forms" truly become human "beings." Ancestral human beings, then, only really come into existence on earth about the middle of the Lemurian Age.

Unfortunately, as the earth accelerated in cooling and solidifying, the physical human bodies were becoming too rigid and inadaptable for the newly-acquired soul vehicle of self-consciousness. In order to properly maintain malleable and amenable conditions on earth for evolving humanity, some of the more densifying and rigidifying etheric forces were spun off to a safer distance from the earth. This enveloping sphere of solidifying and hardening etheric forces would gradually attract dense mineral material to eventually form our present-day moon. These ejected forces have consequently become known as "lunar or moon forces."

Somewhat predictably, the dramatically-changing conditions on earth during the Lemurian Age made it increasingly more impossible for ancestral humanity to continue reproducing by self-fertilization. Consequently, as the lunar forces were gradually distanced from the earth, human physical forms were simultaneously separated into two distinct sexes—male and female. As a result, the etheric male forces of reproduction developed more affinity with the centralizing, centripetal forces of the earth; while the etheric female forces of reproduction developed more affinity with the diffusive, centrifugal forces of the moon. As further explained by Rudolf Steiner in *Cosmic Memory: Prehistory of Earth and Man* (1981):

> In the course of time, the material substances [during the Lemurian Age] become denser; the human body appears in two forms, one of which begins to resemble the subsequent shape of man, the other that of woman ... By becoming male or female, the body lost this possibility of self-impregnation. It had to act together with another body in order to produce a new human being.

> The division into sexes takes place when the earth enters a certain stage of its densification. The density of matter inhibits a portion of the force of reproduction. That portion of this force which is still active needs an external complementation through the opposite force of another human being. The soul however must retain a portion of its earlier energy within itself, in man as well as in woman. It cannot use this portion in the physical external world.

4.3 Sexual Separation and the Development of the Brain

In the second half of the Lemurian Age, after the distancing of the moon from the earth and the consequent separation of the sexes, Lemurian human forms became less animal-like and more human-like in appearance. The lunar distancing of rigidifying etheric forces, for example, enabled the animal-like Lemurians to stand more erect, and to move about in a more upright position.

Also during this time, a large continent formed in the area of the earth now occupied by the Indian Ocean that was much more hospitable to evolving humanity. Having fewer tectonic upheavals and volcanic eruptions, the continent of Lemuria enabled nomadic, ancestral humanity to begin developing stable settlements with cultural refinements such as rudimentary education, farming and animal domestication.

The separation of the sexes also provided a profound and far-reaching evolutionary catalyst for Lemurian humanity. Since males and females were both physically determined by outwardly directing and incorporating *only one* of the gender forces necessary for reproduction, the residual gender forces could be turned inwardly to transform specific organs. In this case, the residual reproductive forces transformed the larynx to enable articulated speech; and also developed the large, outer cerebrum of the brain to enable higher thought processes, physical sense perception and language formation. Once again, as further elaborated by Rudolf Steiner:

> Thus man could use a portion of the energy which previously he employed for the production of beings like himself, in order to perfect his own nature. The force by which mankind forms a thinking brain for itself is the same by which man impregnated himself in ancient times. The price of thought is single-sexedness. By no longer impregnating themselves, but rather by impregnating each other, human beings can turn a part of their productive energy within, and so become thinking creatures. Thus the male and the female body each represent an imperfect external embodiment of the soul, but thereby they become more perfect inwardly. (Ibid.)

4.4   The Progressive Moon-Beings, Human Heredity and Reproduction

From a spiritual perspective, the separation of the moon from the earth during the Lemurian Age was not simply a meaningless physical effect of blind, mechanical forces.

Neither was the sexual separation of our androgynous Lemurian ancestors. Both significant events were under the direction of highly-advanced celestial beings, particularly the powers (or elohim) and the lunar angels. The leading figure involved was the celestial being known biblically as "Yahweh-Elohim." Esoterically understood, Yahweh-Elohim is not the supreme Trinitarian God; but instead is the highest initiate of the angelic kingdom who has advanced to the level of an elohim-power.

Prior to the physical separation of the sexes in ancestral humanity, animal life-forms had already developed sexual reproduction. Unfortunately at that time, the biological boundary between human and animal was not as sharply delineated and exclusionary as it is now. Consequently, humans began crossbreeding with primitive animals, resulting in grotesque, misshapen life-forms. There is, then, in human primordial history an element of truth to the half-human/half-animal creatures depicted in ancient mythology; such as the minotaur, centaur, satyr, harpy and sphinx.

To put an effective halt to this degenerate misuse of reproductive life-forces, Yahweh-Elohim and the lunar angels established the biological laws of heredity.[20] These laws established enduring order, stability and propriety to human sexual reproduction; thereby preventing any further crossbreeding between humans and animals.

4.5 Luciferic Interference in Human Sexuality and Reproduction

Genuine esotericists are well aware that not only has human evolution throughout history been positively promoted by benevolent celestial beings, but it also has been negatively opposed by malevolent celestial beings. During the Lemurian Age, the primary spirits of opposition were the

Luciferic angels.

The ultimate goal of these retrograde angels (under the direction of their powerful leader, Lucifer) was to entice fledgling humanity away from the earth; and instead, to dreamily occupy a renegade planet of Lucifer's formation within the existing solar system. To accomplish this goal, Lucifer and his angels needed to "free" humanity from the direction and control of Yahweh-Elohim and his progressive lunar-angels.

To do this, the Luciferic angels covertly and seductively slipped into the astral bodies of nascent Lemurian humanity; thereby implanting feelings, passions and desires that were contrary to the direction of the progressive lunar-angels. Unfortunately, this corruption and coarsening of the astral body caused a corresponding densification and solidification of the physical body as well.

The unhappy consequence for succeeding generations of human beings was that the physical body became much more deeply enmeshed in chemical, material substance than was originally intended by humanity's wise overseers. The invisible ethereal body with only a loose attachment to chemical matter—that was intended to happily waft about in the earth's atmosphere—instead gradually "fell" to the earth's surface; thereby materializing into a corporeal body of flesh, blood and bone.

Because of this Luciferically-inspired descent into materiality, this primordial "fall from paradise" (known biblically as "original sin" and the "expulsion from Eden") gave rise to pain, sorrow, disease, debilitation and death. In other words, Lucifer's selfish plan to make mankind prematurely "free and independent" has brought untold suffering and misery instead.

Down through the ages and up to the present-day, Lucifer and his angels have continued their relentless assault on humanity. For most of this time, Yahweh-Elohim and the lunar-angels have used the twin strategies of heredity and consanguinity ("blood relations") to keep humanity properly tethered to earth evolution; thereby preventing any illicit Luciferic abduction towards an extra-terrestrial existence.

Contrarily, in a continuous effort to establish premature independence for humanity, Lucifer and his angels have historically opposed family ties and tribal associations based on blood relations. Not only have they repeatedly incited consanguineous family and tribal breakdown, but they've also assailed consanguineous marriage between men and women by encouraging extra-marital sexuality and sexual perversions (such as bestiality, incest, necrophilia, pedophilia and pederasty).

4.6 Male and Female Attraction: From Physical Love to Spiritual Love

As previously emphasized in Chapter 1, the universal masculine principle and the universal feminine principle always operate together. Throughout the cosmos, then, there is never the activity of the one principle without the activity of the other. In a very real sense, both principles can be viewed as the conjoined polar opposites of a single overarching principle—the "principle of universal creation."

There is, therefore, an inherent mutual attraction of the one principle for the other: the masculine principle is attracted to the feminine principle; and the feminine principle is attracted to the masculine principle. In fact, it is this mutual attraction that keeps both principles in perfect harmony and balance.

So for example, under normal circumstances, the masculine principle is only able to inwardly contract so far before the feminine principle is attractively engaged; thereby reversing the direction of movement toward an outer periphery. Likewise, the feminine principle is only able to outwardly expand so far before the masculine principle is attractively engaged; thereby reversing the direction of movement toward an inner centre.

It is, therefore, this mutual attraction that keeps each polarizing principle from going to an extreme. When each gender principle is perfectly operating, they each maintain a state of harmonious equilibrium.

While the two gender principles operate in a more mechanical, impersonal way at the atomic and chemical levels, at the human level they are much more alive and personal. Moreover, since both universal gender principles are a mirrored reflection of the supernal love between the divine masculine person (the Heavenly Father) and the divine feminine person (the Holy Mother), every manifestation in the cosmos—no matter how small or great—expresses a certain degree of divine love.

Predictably, then, with the separation of the sexes in human evolution, there is an inherent, mutual attraction between males and females. This attraction, of course, manifests somewhat differently on the various levels of bodily refinement. On the physical level, for example, gender attraction manifests as the anatomy of sexual distinction and reproduction. On the etheric level, gender attraction manifests as the hormonal and procreative life-processes. On the astral level, gender attraction subconsciously manifests as various instinctual feelings, passions and desires towards physically procreating with the opposite sex. On the lower soul level, gender attraction manifests more selectively as feelings of sensual love towards members of the opposite sex who have a consanguine connection of family, tribe or race. On the upper soul level, gender attraction manifests as a deeper, more-refined and romantic love towards members of the opposite sex who share similar soul configurations (regardless of family, tribe or race). Lastly, on the spiritual level, gender attraction within the context of sacramental marriage manifests as a reverential bond of transcendent love that eternally unites the spiritual selves of husband and wife in the company of God.

Spiritual love is understood at this level to be the mutual, unconditional love that is centred on the other person, and which transcends the personal love of self. Spiritual love is also seen to transcend the boundary of sacramental marriage, and can be universally directed towards all beings, creatures and life-forms. The universality of spiritual love was biblically conveyed by Christ-Jesus, as follows:

> But I say to you, Love your enemies and pray for those who persecute you, so that you may be sons of your Father who is in heaven; for he makes his sun rise on the evil and on the good, and sends rain on the just and on the unjust. For if you love those who love you, what reward have you? Do not even the tax collectors do the same? And if you salute only your brethren, what more are you doing than others? Do not even the Gentiles do the same? You, therefore, must be perfect, as your heavenly Father is perfect. (Matt 5:44–48)

As here indicated by our Saviour, spiritual love is a reflection of divine love—the perfect love of God—which shines on the true being of all persons; even those who choose to oppose him.

4.7 The Assault on Spiritual Love by the Powers of Darkness

Unfortunately, there are beings—human and celestial—who deliberately defy and willingly oppose God and all his heavenly messengers. And since God's spirit-nature is divine love, these various "beings of opposition" (also collectively referred to as "spirits of darkness") predictably target and work to destroy all human knowledge, expression and experience of spiritual love.

In the case of Lucifer, one of the foremost spirits of darkness, his long-term strategy has been to promote "self-love" as a replacement for "love of the other." For this reason, Lucifer can well be described as the preeminent "cosmic narcissist." For long ages of earth evolution, Lucifer has exemplified and promoted a hedonistic, self-centred and egotistical form of love—and continues to do so today.

Moreover, Lucifer's nefarious activity is further characterized as being a deliberate distortion of the universal feminine principle. By expanding outwardly to an extreme degree, Lucifer knowingly extends beyond the proper boundary of harmonious balance into an aberrant condition of attenuated delusion.

Using human knowledge as an example, Lucifer will exaggerate true facts to cosmic proportions; thereby distorting their actual meaning. He quite literally strives to "stretch the truth" in order to create his own false reality. Using human love as an example, Lucifer will over-inflate and hyperbolize the pleasures of physical, sensual love in an attempt to replace true transcendent love with an exaggerated counterfeit.

An additional spirit of darkness, known as Ahriman (or Satan), also strives to destroy all human knowledge, expression and experience of spiritual love—but in a manner opposite to Lucifer. Ahriman's malevolent activity is characterized as being a deliberate distortion of the universal masculine principle. By contracting inwardly to an extreme degree, Ahriman constricts beyond the proper boundary of harmonious balance; in this case into an aberrant condition of anamorphic compression.

As a consequence, Ahriman continually attempts to pull the spiritual down to the level of the physical; that is, to condense, densify and solidify rarified spirituality into coarse materiality. Regarding mankind, Ahriman works to annihilate any awareness of a spiritual connection; thereby reducing human beings to the level of intelligent animals. Under Ahriman's influence, then, spiritual love is coarsened and debased to the level of crude animal instinct.

A third powerful spirit of darkness who has been historically driven to destroy all human knowledge, expression and experience of spiritual love is Sorath, the sun demon. From his hellish confinement at the centre of the earth, Sorath exerts what influence he can to destroy the balanced equilibrium and harmony between the two universal genders.

In regard to humanity, then, Sorath fuels a "gender war" between men and women; attempting to destroy the inherent complementarity and mutuality of the two sexes. Even more maliciously, he instills violence, brutality, cruelty, savagery and blood-lust into the sexual relations between men and women. Sorath, then, is the evil inspiration behind sadism, masochism, bondage, domination, rape and ritual killing. In short, this demonic spirit of darkness seeks to curtail the gradual unfoldment of spiritual love in human beings by inspiring, instilling and encouraging every conceivable sexual deviance and perversion. Moreover, since Christ-Jesus is the pre-eminent instiller and promoter of spiritual love within humanity, Sorath is his avowed and foremost enemy.

4.8   Future Female Sterility and Reproduction by the Word

Just as in the primordial past our animal-like ancestors were capable of reproducing by self-fertilization without being sexually separated, so there will similarly come a time in the not-too-distant future when our angel-like descendents will once again become capable of self-fertilization without being sexually separated—but in an entirely different way of course.

The clairvoyant research of Rudolf Steiner has indicated that by the sixth millennium, radical transformations on earth[21] will cause women to become increasingly infertile.[22] Moreover, the gradual separation of the etheric body from the physical will also necessitate the development of a new process of human reproduction.

As shocking and unbelievable as it appears to current understanding and experience, future self-fertilization will occur through the interaction of a transformed heart and a transformed larynx. In other words, the metamorphosed heart and larynx will become the reproductive organs of the future.

Though precise details of the future method of self-fertilization have not been publicly conveyed as yet, there is enough general information currently available to gather a rough conception.[23] At present, the larynx is capable of shaping the external substance of air in accordance with internal thoughts and ideas; that is, it is able to formulate word-sounds.

In the future, the feminine life-forces working through the heart and larynx, together with the masculine forces of the will, will be capable of externally generating a living human-form out of etheric substance that is able to attract physical material; and thereby provide an incarnational vehicle for an incoming soul. Expressed more succinctly, in the future, human reproduction will be accomplished through the "power of the word." As conveyed by Rudolf Steiner in a lecture given on 05 June 1907 entitled "The Future of Man":

> The generative process and all that stands in connection with it will pass over in the future to another organ. The organ that is already preparing to become the future organ of generation is the human larynx. Today it can

only bring forth vibrations of the air, can only impart to the air what lies in the word that goes forth from it, so that the vibrations correspond to the word. Later on, not only will the word press forward in its rhythm from the larynx, but it will be irradiated by man, it will be penetrated by very substance. Just as today the word only becomes airwaves, so in the future man's inner being, his own likeness, which today is in his word, will issue from the larynx. The human being will proceed from the human being, man will *speak forth* man. And this in the future will be the birth of a new human being—that he is spoken forth by another. (Published in *Theosophy of the Rosicrucian*; 1966)

As outlandish as the notion of "reproduction by the word" may initially appear to the novice seeker, informed esotericists are familiar with the already-acquired ability of highly-advanced initiates to perpetuate their physical existence on earth for numerous centuries by fashioning for themselves new etheric bodies. The future method of self-generation through the word is simply the collective development and acquisition of this vestigial initiate-ability.

CHAPTER 5

SUPERNATURAL FACTORS UNDERLYING THE SEXUAL REVOLUTION

5.1 The Age of the Consciousness Soul and Freedom from Authority

HOW IS IT that for thousands of years of human history, it was an unquestioned, self-evident truth that there existed only two distinct sexes—male and female—and that men and women were naturally attracted to each other, choosing to unite into stable family units for the purposes of spousal union and the procreation of children? Why is there today an increasing number of people who either question or reject these foundational principles of human behaviour and of human society?

The healthy, progressive and consistent expression of human sexuality throughout the ages has been entirely due to the wise guidance, regulation and control of this crucial life-function by Yahweh-Elohim and his faithful moon-angels (including the archangel Gabriel). The divinely-intended purpose of human sexuality was guaranteed by mankind's celestial overseers in two principal ways.

Firstly, strict moral laws, customs and traditions concerning human sexuality were socially established by divinely-inspired religious leaders. Secondly, several powerful instincts concerning human sexuality were subconsciously instilled into the astral bodies of nascent mankind—instincts such as the strong attraction to the opposite sex; the imperative instinct to mate (marry), to procreate and to establish an enduring family unit; the forceful instinct to protect one's spouse and children; and the compelling instinct to identify with one's biological sex.

Similar to the animal kingdom today, for long ages prehistoric humanity unquestioningly obeyed these powerful, subconscious instincts. But as human beings increasingly developed self-conscious awareness and free-will, these instincts became less and less compulsory in nature. While the vast majority of human beings continue to subconsciously conform to these healthy and beneficent sexual instincts, more and more individuals today are beginning to vaguely question, to intellectually reject or even to behaviourally disobey them.

Moreover, the increased weakening of instinctual imperatives is consonant with the spirit of our modern age. According to esoteric science, what is loosely-termed, "The Renaissance," was actually the beginning of an entirely new cultural era of human development. The "Anglo-European" cultural era began in 1413 and is destined to last until 3573.[24]

Since the final submergence of the continent and civilization of Atlantis, there have been four previous cultural eras: (1) the "ancient Indian" (7227–5067 BC), (2) the "ancient Persian" (5067–2907 BC), (3) the "Egypto–Chaldean" (2907–747 BC), and (4) the "Graeco-Roman" (747 BC–1413).

Each cultural era is destined to concentrate on and further develop one of humanity's many interpenetrating vehicles of expression (see Figure 6 below).

COSMIC REALMS OF EXISTENCE	INDIVIDUAL LEVELS OF EXISTENCE	VEHICLES OF EXPRESSION	EGO (SELF)	SANSKRIT TERMS	DEGREES OF CONSCIOUSNESS
CELESTIAL WORLD [SPIRIT LAND]	SPIRIT	SPIRIT-BODY	THE HIGHER	ATMAN	DIVINE CONSCIOUSNESS
	SPIRIT	LIFE-SPIRIT	THE HIGHER	BUDDHI	COSMIC CONSCIOUSNESS
	SPIRIT	SPIRIT-SELF	THE HIGHER	MANAS	SPIRITUAL CONSCIOUSNESS
SOUL WORLD	SOUL	CONSCIOUSNESS SOUL			SOUL CONSCIOUSNESS
	SOUL	INTELLECTUAL SOUL	THE LOWER	KAMA-RUPA	SELF CONSCIOUSNESS
	SOUL	SENTIENT SOUL	THE LOWER		WAKING CONSCIOUSNESS
PHYSICAL WORLD	BODY	ASTRAL BODY		LINGA-SHARIRA	DREAM CONSCIOUSNESS
	BODY	ETHERIC BODY		PRANA-JIVA	SLEEP CONSCIOUSNESS
	BODY	PHYSICAL BODY		STHULA-SHARIRA	TRANCE CONSCIOUSNESS

Figure 6: Humanity's Vehicles of Expression

The Egypto-Chaldean cultural era, for example, further developed the sentient soul vehicle; while the Graeco-Roman cultural era further developed the intellectual soul vehicle. The current Anglo-European cultural era is destined to further develop the consciousness (or spiritualized) soul vehicle

During the previous cultural eras, progressive development was effectively achieved through the power of authority. During that time, small numbers of divinely-inspired leaders directed, educated and slowly advanced the vast throng of undeveloped humanity by employing their authoritative social position and forceful influence.

Our present-day cultural era, however, has the destiny of laying the foundation of free and independent intellectual thought without any undue reliance on external sources of authority. While the full fruition of "free thinking" is destined to occur during the sixth post-Atlantean cultural era, the foundational seeds are being sown in our own modern era.

In consequence, more and more individuals today are beginning to question the long-held traditional ideas and beliefs concerning human sexuality; even to the point of questioning their own basic sexual instincts (such as the strong innate attraction to the opposite sex, for example).

5.2   The Rise of Atheism and Secular Society in Modern Times

The present-day predilection to intellectually challenge any and all sources of authority, and to readily dismiss all prior tradition and orthodoxy has resulted in an increasing rejection of the ultimate authority figure—Almighty God. Before the present age of "free-thinking" and "skeptical inquiry," virtually every human being believed in a supreme God, a pantheon of multiple gods, or a hierarchy of supernatural beings.

Consequently, all societies in the past were "sacred societies," social arrangements that were characterized by an unquestioning belief and interconnection with the spiritual world. A disbelief in God; that is—"atheism"—is a very recent ideological aberration. Likewise, the present-day heterodox notion of a completely "secular society"; that is, an atheistically-inclined social order where religious institutions are denigrated, marginalized and disregarded is also a recent mental fabrication.

Clearly, the irreligious notions of atheism and secular society are Ahrimanically-inspired strategies to drive all knowledge and awareness of spiritual reality (particularly God) from human experience. If God is no longer understood to be the only true reality, then non-believers feel free to establish their own pseudo-realities—such as deciding their own eccentric definition of sexual identity; or their own peculiar definition of marriage; or their own non-traditional definition of family; or their own inverted definition of normalcy.

Moreover, if God is no longer understood to be the one true source of moral goodness and ethical truth, then non-believers feel freely emboldened to concoct their own idiosyncratic systems of right and wrong;[25] or to unabashedly ignore all moral consideration regarding their own behaviour. By willfully rejecting the existence of an absolute moral authority (God) behind all creation, personal behaviour very quickly declines towards an attitude of "anything goes," and the social order soon degenerates into becoming a "permissive society."

In the area of human sexuality, increasingly-permissive secular societies pronounce less and less moral judgement on all manner of sexual deviation and perversion. In many Western societies today, the "liberal" attitude has become "anything goes as long as it's done in private, and/or between consenting adults."[26]

5.3 Materialistic Science and the Purpose of Human Sexuality

By intellectually abolishing God and the spiritual world from human experience, atheism and secular society effectively remove any consideration of "purpose" to human behaviour and cosmic activity. If there is no underlying divine, omniscient Creator, then there can be no intelligent design or purpose to any life-form or chemical activity within the universe.

The aberrant notion that the universe is entirely purposeless is also bolstered by present-day materialistic (or "empirical") science. Not surprisingly, since materialistic science exclusively restricts its study and investigations to the lifeless realm of physical matter and energy, it can find no innate purpose or underlying meaning there. That's because intelligent purpose to physical matter and energy throughout the universe is established at a much higher, spiritual level.

Materialistic science, therefore, astonishingly rejects even such obvious, common-sense, self-evident truths as "the purpose of the eye is to see" or "the purpose of the ear is to hear." Not surprisingly, then, materialistic science also rejects the obvious, common-sense, self-evident truth that there is a purpose to human sexuality. Aside from the loving intimacy of husband and wife, the obvious purpose of human sexuality is the procreation of children—without which present-day humanity could not continue to exist on earth.

By negating any purpose to human sexuality, adherents of today's materialistic science can treat it as just another animalistic appetite that needs to be regularly satisfied—as just another bodily itch that needs to be scratched. The ecstatic joy that rightly comes from marital intimacy and the procreation of new life is thereby denigrated to a lust for selfish erotic pleasure. And of course without a divinely-intended purpose, the sexual itch can be scratched in any number of degenerate ways—bestiality, bondage, rape, incest, auto-eroticism or sado-masochism.

Moreover, when procreation is not acknowledged as a prime purpose of human sexuality, then pregnancy is viewed as an undesirable side-effect of pleasure-seeking sexual activity. Contraception and abortion are therefore celebrated as welcomed antidotes to the nasty sexual by-product of pregnancy.

From an esoteric point of view, then, modern materialistic science is another effective, Ahrimanically-inspired method of eradicating any knowledge of God and the spiritual world from human experience. Unfortunately as well, many of the technologies that have developed out of materialistic science also direct human attention away from God and the spiritual world, and focus it on the physical world instead.

Ahrimanically-inspired technology has certainly contributed to today's sexual revolution (or "devolution"). For example, the current flirtation with "transgenderism"—the strong desire to change one's anatomical sex—would certainly not be possible without the discovery of hormone replacement therapy, together with the development of new sex-reassignment surgical techniques. And of course the "free love" component of the sexual revolution (that is, the "freedom" to have sexual intercourse without the risk of pregnancy) was enormously accelerated and expanded by the development of the birth-control pill in the 1960s.

5.4 Collectively Crossing the Threshold: The Separation of Thinking, Feeling and Willing

An additional, subconscious contributing factor to the current upheaval in human sexuality and gender is the clairvoyantly observable fact that mankind has collectively entered the lower etheric realm. The etheric realm is the invisible, supersensible world closest to the physical. What we know and experience as physical heat and light are, in fact, energy-vibrations in the ether. As the ultra-rarified medium for the transmission of energy waves, ether is similar to the Einsteinian notion of "physical space." But unlike physical space, ether is esoterically understood to have four distinct gradations: (1) warmth ether, (2) light ether, (3) tone or chemical ether and (4) life ether. It is the formative forces of the life ether that direct, maintain and sustain the life-form and life-activity of the physical body.

Throughout the Lemurian and most of the Atlantean Ages, the etheric body—particularly the etheric head—partially hovered outside the periphery of the physical body. By the last third of the Atlantean Age, however, the two bodies had gradually become synchronously aligned, particularly at a central point in the head between the eyebrows. Such an alignment was evolutionarily necessary in order to develop physical sensory perception, together with increased self-awareness.[27]

Since the beginning of the Anglo-European cultural era in 1413, however, the etheric body has begun to gradually withdraw from the physical body. In consequence, between 1842 and 1879, mankind as a whole unconsciously and unknowingly crossed the threshold into the etheric realm. As occurs in the individual, conscious process of initiation, the collective passage into the supersensible world also causes the gradual separation of the conjoined soul-forces of thinking, feeling and willing.[28]

Unfortunately, without the conscious awareness of this soul-force separation and the crucial need to freely re-establish a new soul-harmony from a higher (Christ) consciousness, the vast majority of mankind begins to gradually descend into an unconscious state of psychotic delusion.[29] One can disturbingly observe this growing psychopathology covertly spreading into all aspects of human life, including the understanding, valuation and expression of human sexuality.

5.5 Manipulation of Sexuality and Reproduction by the Spirits of Darkness since 1879

Since the primordial dawn of humanity during the Lemurian Age, human sexuality has been strictly and wisely regulated by benevolent spiritual overseers, particularly Yahweh-Elohim and the progressive lunar-angels. The laws governing genetics, heredity and sexual reproduction beneficially anchored struggling humanity to earth evolution; thereby counteracting evil Luciferic endeavours to seduce mankind away from the earth.

As well, social arrangements such as families, tribes and nations were universally based on blood relationships as a means of experiencing human love in its rudimentary, parochial form. During this time, the Luciferic spirits vehemently opposed all forms of collective blood-relationships; and instead promoted a beguiling, pseudo-independence based on a self-centred, narcissistic form of love.

Throughout the long ages, strict social taboos and powerful subconscious instincts astrally implanted by humanity's celestial guardians provided harmonious order and beneficial permanence to human sexuality, reproduction and consanguineous love. However, this important and necessary phase of human development began to be gradually transformed and superseded during the Graeco-Roman cultural era due to the world-altering incarnation of divine love in Christ-Jesus.

Hereafter, the progressive celestial beings, now under the evolutionary direction of Christ-Jesus, no longer promoted human relations, loyalties and affections based on hereditary blood-lines; but strove instead to encourage free and independent associations of human beings based on the principle of universal love.

Moreover, in assisting Christ-Jesus in properly unfolding the individualized spiritual-self within each human soul—together with the increased capacity of free-will choice—the lunar angels of procreation have increasingly loosened their powerful instinctive control of human sexuality and reproduction. Consequently, more and more present-day human beings are acquiring the free-will capacity to ignore or disregard these once-commanding sexual instincts. Today, therefore, it is much easier to depress the strong, innate instinct of attraction to the opposite sex; and thereby entertain the once-adverse notion of erotic relations with the same sex.

Not surprisingly, once the progressive lunar angels—the "spirits of light"— began to gradually relinquish instinctual control of human sexuality and the hidden laws of heredity, regressive supernatural beings—the "spirits of darkness"—quickly moved in to usurp control. Where throughout the ancient past Luciferic spirits relentlessly laboured to "free" individual human beings from all hereditary social connections based on blood-lines, and thereby make them "independent individualities," since the beginning of the Anglo-European cultural era in 1413 these same Luciferic spirits are now doing the exact opposite.[30]

Today's Luciferic spirits are directing human attention backwards to the outmoded tribal and racial conditions of the past; thereby fomenting sectarian hatred and warfare between various ethnic groups. Such is clearly the case with the tribal violence currently raging in the Middle East and in other parts of the world.

Moreover, in addition to promoting a pseudo-spiritual ego that is independent of God, today's Luciferic spirits are also regressively using the group-identity of archaic tribalism[31] to thwart progressive, fully-conscious spirit-self development, and replace it with a dreamy, semi-conscious "oneness with nature self-identity" instead. Such is clearly the case today with the various New Age-style practices that deaden healthy ego-awareness in favour of a "warm and fuzzy," somnolent collective-selfhood.

Unfortunately, since 1879, the assault against human sexuality by the spirits of darkness has rapidly intensified. In the fall of 1879, as indicated by the esoteric research of Rudolf Steiner, the spirits of light led by St. Michael prevailed against a determined horde of dark-spirits in a protracted war in heaven. Briefly summarized, since the mid-nineteenth century the spirits of darkness—in this case certain Ahrimanic beings—had attempted to eclipse the entire etheric realm of the earth with dense materialistic forces. This nefarious assault was successfully repelled by the celestial forces of St. Michael. In consequence, these rebellious Ahrimanic beings were "cast out of heaven," and banished to the lower-etheric realm of the earth.

The positive outcome of this victory by the supernatural forces of light was that intellectual access to the spiritual world was now easier to attain for human beings. The downside, unfortunately, was that many more inimical Ahrimanic beings now moved etherically amongst unwary humanity; thereby gaining increased influence over materialistic thinking.

Predictably, this newly-displaced, earth-bound horde of Ahrimanic beings quickly began targeting human sexuality as a way of furthering their evil intentions for the earth. Unlike the Luciferic beings who passionately strive to seduce humanity away from the earth, the Ahrimanic beings calculatingly conspire to permanently chain feckless humanity to the earth as glorified, spiritless, animal-like creatures.

Since 1879, Ahrimanically-inspired materialistic science has succeeded in cracking the once spiritually-guarded genetic code and the long-hidden secrets of human reproduction. Through genetic engineering, today's impetuous scientists are recklessly toying with powerful reproductive forces, and have already opening up a Pandora's Box of horrific possibilities.

Present-day scientists have already begun to manipulate the genetic material of various existing life-forms, such as plants and animals, in order to synthesize new, genetically modified organisms (GMOs). Bacteria were the first to be genetically modified in 1973; and by 1974, mice were also being genetically modified. Since 1994, genetically modified food has been produced, marketed and consumed worldwide.

Frightening future possibilities of biotechnical genetic manipulation can be easily projected from the actual artificial generation in early 2000 of "spider-goats"—goats that've had spider genes added to their DNA. This was economically devised so that the goats would produce spider-silk protein in their milk; which can then be extracted to produce a super-strong fibre, coating or adhesive. In the experimental hands of iniquitous and immoral scientists and research institutions, monstrous and malefic creatures (such as deadly bacteria and viruses for military use) could be similarly devised; then inadvertently released on an unsuspecting, unprepared and defenseless human population.

In addition, it is important to be esoterically clear that the earth-bound Ahrimanic beings who have covertly moved amongst humanity since 1879 intend to use genetic manipulation to usurp divinely-instilled human procreation. Their evil intention is to artificially generate a super-intelligent, human-animal creature—a spiritless, biological man-machine. Moreover, by replacing long-established, human sexual procreation with artificial fertility procedures (that is, "assisted reproductive technologies")—such as in-vitro fertilization, surrogacy, intracytoplasmic sperm injection and cryopreservation—the purposeful need for any male and female sexual intercourse would be seriously undermined or even abolished.

CHAPTER 6

ANOMALIES, EXCEPTIONS AND MISCONCEPTIONS CONCERNING HUMAN SEXUALITY

6.1 The Anomalous Condition of Intersexuality

GIVEN THE ASTOUNDING complexity of the human physical body, it is truly amazing that more developmental disorders, irregularities, abnormalities, anomalies, aberrations, deviations and incongruities do not regularly occur. Nevertheless, many do occur, including in the complicated area of human sexuality.

Though the vast majority of human beings are born and develop with a clearly-defined male and female sexual biology, there are rare instances where certain sexual characteristics become developmentally confused and intermingled. The most familiar examples, well-known throughout the ancient world, were termed "hermaphrodites" by the Classical Greeks (from Hermes—a male deity, plus Aphrodite—a female deity). In this case, hermaphrodites atypically combined the external sexual anatomy of male and female (such as female breasts and male genitalia).

Today, human sexuality—as revealed by modern science—is known to be much more multifaceted than simply external anatomy. Biologically, sex is determined by a number of intricate factors, including: (1) the number and type of chromosomes, (2) the type of gonads (ovaries or testicles), (3) the sex hormones, (4) the internal reproductive anatomy (such as the uterus in females) and (5) the external genitalia. Consequently, there are many more developmental possibilities for male and female sex factors to be atypically conjoined.

"Intersex" and "intersexuality" are the current terms used to describe individuals who are born with any of the several anomalous variations in sex characteristics (including chromosomes, gonads, sex hormones, internal reproductive anatomy and genitalia) that do not conform to normally-developed male and female bodies.

A few examples of the wide range of intersexual abnormalities are the following:

(1) "Ovatestis": individuals have both ovarian and testicular tissue; usually with ambiguous genitalia at birth, and breast development at puberty

(2) "Sex Chromosome Mosaicism": individuals have more or less than the normal 46 chromosomes in some of their cells.

(3) "Klinefelter Syndrome": male individuals have a sex chromosome makeup of XXY instead of just XY (also known as XXY Syndrome). Most develop male breasts in puberty, have underdeveloped testes and lack development of normal male secondary sexual characteristics.

(4) "Turner Syndrome": female individuals do not have the normal 46 chromosomes; but instead have 45 with only a single X chromosome. No breast development at puberty, and genitals are usually undeveloped.

(5) "Triple X Syndrome": female individuals have an additional female (X) chromosome in each of their cells. This often results in taller than average height, with increased risk of learning disabilities, delayed development of speech and language skills, delayed development of motor skills, weak muscle tone, and possible behavioral and emotional difficulties.

(6) "Jacobs Syndrome": male individuals have an extra male (Y) chromosome, giving a total of 47 chromosomes instead of the usual 46. This often results in taller than average height, learning difficulties, speech problems, and minor physical differences (such as weaker muscle tone).

(7) "Female Sex Reversal Syndrome": individuals with female chromosomes (XX), and a male chromosome fragment (Y) translocated in their system. This disorder results in a genetic female developing as a male.

(8) "Androgen Insensitivity Syndrome" (AIS): is caused by a genetic error in the androgen receptor (AR) gene on the X chromosome. Individuals with AIS have 46 male chromosomes (XY); but depending on the mutation, may develop as a male, a female, or may have genitalia that are only partially masculinized. Regardless, the gonads are always testes due to the influence of the Y chromosome.

While there are many more intersex anomalies that could be listed and described here, in every case there is an atypical variance from the normal sexual development of male and female. Though it is not unusual for anomalies to occur in nature, this does not mean that these anomalies are "normal" and "natural." The birth of two-headed calves has certainly occurred in nature, for example; but it is irrational to infer that such births are normal and natural.

Likewise with intersexuality, some recent researchers have mistakenly attempted to argue that these "disorders of sex development" (DSDs) are normal and natural. Such attempts appear to be based more on "politically-correct minority-sensitivity" than on actual biology. In order to avoid any social regard that intersex individuals are somehow "different" than the rest of male and female society, misguided advocates have attempted to disregard, ignore or alter the biological reality that they are. In the words of pediatrician and geneticist, Eric Vilain:

> [I]ntermediate states between the different biological sexes are extremely rare and often associated with infertility, which in evolutionary terms consigns them to a dead end ... It is not reasonable to place the two biological sexes present in the vast majority of cases on the same level as the extremely rare intermediate sexes.[31]

A similar misguided sympathy also appears to explain the illogical notion that intersexuality constitutes a separate and distinct "third sex." As previously stated, the various expressions of intersexuality are in every instance the abnormal comingling of male and female sex factors. The two sexes have been divinely and biologically established primarily for procreation; a third sex is not necessary, and therefore does not exist.

Regardless of developmental aberrations, the division of humanity into two clearly-defined and mutually-complementary sexes is a clear biological fact, and not simply "arbitrary gender stereotypes," or the "male-female binary theory of biological sex," or "socially-constructed gender roles," or a "social convention of human anatomy," or a "Platonic ideal of sexual dimorphism," or a "Judeo-Christian religious belief," or "feminine and masculine gender-norms," or "patriarchal divisions of dominance (men) and submission (women)."

While efforts to address issues of intersex discrimination and stigmatization are commendable, it is not beneficial to undertake radical biological revisionism in order to advance social sensibility and awareness. Thankfully, it's not only religion and esoteric science that reject the aberrant notion of a third sex, or of multiple sexes—sane voices in the scientific and medical communities also concur. According to the American College of Pediatricians:

> Human sexuality is an objective biological binary trait: 'XY' and 'XX' are genetic markers of health—not genetic markers of a disorder. The norm for human design is to be conceived either male or female. Human sexuality is binary by design with the obvious purpose being the reproduction and flourishing of our species. This principle is self-evident ... Individuals with DSDs (disorders of sex development) do not constitute a third sex.

6.2   Homosexuality and Same-Sex Attraction

Given that human sexuality has been divinely ordained and biologically ordered for the purposes of marital intimacy and for the procreation and raising of children, it is logically obvious that there is a strong, innate sexual attraction between men and women. Sexual attraction to the same sex (as a whole)[32] obviously runs counter to the evolutionary survivability of humanity; and is, therefore, an uncommon, atypical and anomalous desire.

Due to well-funded and well-organized political activism in Western countries since the 1960s, the prevalence of homosexuality appears much greater to public perception than it actual is. Gallup poll figures compiled in 2017 by recognized demographer, Gary J. Gates, indicated that only 4.1% of Americans in 2016 identified as being homosexual (that is, "LGBT" = lesbian, gay, bisexual and transgender).

In other words, in a modern-day, liberalized Western country with wide social acceptance, the vast majority of Americans—95.9%—still indicated a definitive sexual attraction to the opposite sex (heterosexuality). No doubt the small percentage of self-identified homosexuals in America would be even smaller worldwide, due to over 70 countries where homosexuality is still illegal.

Statistically then—despite the claims of LGBT activists and their "progressive liberal" supporters in the media, government, academia, medical profession and scientific community—it is obvious that heterosexuality is the norm, and that homosexuality is a clear deviation from the norm.[33] Homosexuality, then, is a clear deviation from the dominantly-natural reproductive attraction to the opposite sex. As such, by definition it is non-natural and non-normative. As previously indicated with intersexuality, the fact that homosexuality has occurred in small numbers throughout history does not logically or scientifically establish that it is normal and natural.

While same-sex attraction (SSA) clearly runs counter to the dominant, instinctual attraction to the opposite sex, this does not mean that homosexual persons do not adhere to other deep-seated sexual instincts; such as the desire to be married, the desire for a loving relationship, the desire for sexual intimacy, the desire to raise children, and the desire to establish a loving family. In other words, though LGBT persons express an uncommon same-sex attraction, this does not necessarily imply that they do not share many other strong, deep-seated, instinctive sexual desires that are commonly adhered to by heterosexual persons.

Given that same-sex attraction is anomalous and runs counter to normal human sexuality, and given that most individuals are instinctively repelled at the thought of erotic relations with their own sex, what accounts for its persistence throughout history?

While there is no single, definitive determinant, there are a number of reasonable explanations that can be considered here. For instance, some theorists have suggested that there are biological factors that contribute to homosexuality, such as genetics, hormones and fetal development. Others suggest a complex combination of biological and environmental (including psychological and sociological) factors. While there has been no conclusive scientific evidence thus far, certain individuals clearly demonstrate homosexual tendencies at an early age.

Nevertheless, despite what some theorists contend, not every homosexual person was born with same-sex attraction; in many instances it is definitely a matter of choice—evidenced by the fact that some heterosexual persons have chosen a homosexual lifestyle later in life; while some homosexual persons have discontinued their lifestyle and become heterosexual.

So the question now is: why would individuals throughout history choose not to adhere to the powerful reproductive instinct of attraction to the opposite sex? There are, of course, a number of very practical reasons that can be offered here. One very common inducement is the prolonged lack of contact with the opposite sex. When individuals are exclusively surrounded by members of their own sex for extended periods of time, the powerful instinct for sexual intimacy can be unnaturally diverted. Such has historically been the case for young men and women in private schools and academies, men in the military, women in harems, and men and women in prison.

Another possible reason for same-sex attraction is a developed aversion or fear of the opposite sex due to physical, emotional, mental or sexual abuse; traumatic childhood experiences such as rape or incest; and instances of torture during war, terrorism or kidnapping. In consequence, painfully-affected individuals may turn to their own sex in order to satisfy the powerful need for sexual intimacy.

In some instances, same-sex attraction is just a temporary phase of curiosity and experimentation. Studies have indicated, for example, that half of the American teenagers who identified as being homosexual did not continue to do so later in life. Since the intensity of puberty is experienced during the adolescent years, it is quite understandable that some naive and rebellious erotic experimentation can occur as sexual identity is developmentally solidified. In the case of adults, after the pain of a long and difficult marital breakup, divorcées may temporarily flirt with same-sex attraction in order to decide whether a future homosexual relationship is preferable to the previously-unpleasant heterosexual one.[34]

The 2017 Gallup poll referred to earlier rather predictably found that American millennials (those born between 1980 and 1998) were more than twice as likely as any other generation to identify as homosexual (LGBT). As well, millennials accounted for more than half (58%) of total identified American homosexuals.

Clearly the increase in self-identified homosexuals among American millennials was not because more homosexuals were suddenly born between 1980 and 1998, but because of personal choice. Millennials tend to be politically-socialist[35] (and support same-sex marriage, marijuana legalization and identity-politics); not strong practitioners of traditional religion; strongly concerned with political-correctness (such as microaggressions, trigger warnings and safe spaces[36]); and less interested in marriage and having children than previous generations. Moreover, since American millennials have been nurtured on movies, television, books, magazines, pride parades, academic studies and university courses supportive of homosexuality, they are far more likely to consider a homosexual lifestyle as a "personal choice" than would the previous generations.

Whatever the reasons for same-sex attraction, for the vast majority of persons worldwide the attraction to the opposite sex and the desire to procreate is instinctually built into the human psyche and physiology. In other words, attraction to the opposite sex—also referred to as "sexual orientation"—and the desire to procreate are biologically and psychologically pre-established; they are not a matter of choice for most heterosexual persons. The question is, therefore: "Is same-sex attraction similarly pre-established for certain individuals?"

In terms of esoteric science, attraction to the opposite sex is a compelling subconscious desire that was implanted in the astral body by advanced celestial beings during humanity's primordial past. It was deliberately made powerfully irresistible because the survivability of humanity depends on sexual reproduction; that is, on the attraction between opposite sexes—male and female.

Same-sex attraction, then, is an anomalous desire that runs counter to the divinely-intended one. As such, it is not necessary for human survivability; and therefore lacks the same powerfully-instinctive compulsion. However, since homosexual persons possess the same reproductive biology as heterosexual persons, they potentially have the same powerfully-instinctive desire to procreate. Unfortunately, successful procreation can never result from the sexual activity between persons of the same sex. For many homosexual persons, however, having children is not the goal of sexual activity; but rather, erotic pleasure or sexual intimacy.

In the view of esoteric science, then, same-sex attraction is simply a non-normative, non-natural desire; it is not a mental illness (as previously claimed by the medical profession). Since it has not been instinctually implanted by humanity's celestial overseers, same-sex attraction—as a desire—can be effectively supplanted over time with a normal heterosexual attraction. Such a modification of sexual orientation would only be positive and successful if it is entirely the free-will choice—and not one that was forced or coerced—of the homosexual person involved.

Aside from an anomalous same-sex attraction, since many homosexual persons respond to the same instinctual needs and desires as heterosexual persons, they naturally strive for similar treatment under the law regarding marital rights, adoption rights, anti-discrimination legislation and equal opportunity in the workplace. Many of these individuals have formed stable, long-lasting relationships and positive, child-rearing family units.

Other homosexuals, however, pride themselves on being different than heterosexuals; and therefore promote a separate homosexual lifestyle referred to as "gay" or "queer culture." Those who subscribe to queer culture very often perpetuate the stereotype of being openly and admittedly promiscuous, extravagant and flamboyant in dress and behaviour, and overtly disdainful of social convention and decorum.

Unfortunately, it is primarily this particular homosexual population that is at increased risk of suicide, eating disorders, substance misuse, and breast and anal cancer. For example, about 70% of Americans with AIDS are male homosexuals, and up to 86% of homosexual males use various drugs to enhance and increase their sexual stimulation. Homosexuals in general are three times more suicidal than heterosexuals, and the life expectancy of both homosexual men and women—without AIDS—is significantly shorter than that of heterosexuals.

6.3 Transgenderism and Sexual Identity Confusion

Where homosexuality is an anomalous condition of "sexual orientation," transgenderism is an anomalous condition of "sexual identity." Sexual identity is simply the psychological (mental and emotional) affirmation of being physiologically male or female. As with sexual orientation (that is, attraction to the opposite sex), for the vast majority of human beings sexual identity is instinctually pre-established. In other words, almost everyone psychologically identifies with their own particular physiological sex—those born with a male body naturally consider themselves to be a man; while those born with a female body naturally consider themselves to be woman.

Transgenderism is the rare instance where an individual does not identify with their particular sexual physiology. In other words, a person with a male body psychologically identifies as a woman; and a person with a female body psychologically identifies as a man. Medically, transgenderism continues to be regarded as a disorder; although recently the American Psychiatric Association (APA) changed its designation from "gender identity disorder" (GID) to "gender dysphoria."

While certain mild instances of gender non-conformity (such as men wearing make-up, or women not shaving their legs) are not in themselves mental disorders, transgenderism is an exceptionally-rare extreme. A 2016 survey done by UCLA's Williams Institute estimated that only 0.6% of US adults identify as transgender. Not psychologically recognizing the self-evident fact that if one has a male body, then one is logically a man; or if one has a female body, then one is logically a woman—is an unhealthy denial of reality, and a serious mental disorder.

Unfortunately, in order to satisfy the present-day leftist obsession with political correctness, the medical community has chosen to white-wash the obvious fact that transgenderism is an aberrant mental disorder. In order to misguidedly spare gender-confused individuals from the possibility of negative social repercussions (such as discrimination or harassment), and from negative emotional side-effects (such as depression or anxiety), transgender advocates expect the rest of society to pretend that this mental disorder is both natural and normal.

Since transgenderism is mental confusion concerning one's sexual identity, the obvious remedy is psychotherapy; that is, adjusting one's thinking and feeling to harmoniously correspond with one's physiological sex. Instead, to surgically and hormonally reshape one's sexual anatomy and reproductive system to artificially accommodate one's aberrant thoughts and emotions is decidedly irrational and extreme. Besides, even with such drastic transmutilation, one only has the artificial appearance of the opposite sex—at the genetic and cellular level, one's original biological sex remains entirely unchanged.

The alarmingly-high rate of attempted suicide among transgender individuals is clear evidence that drastic sex-reassignment surgery and cross-sex hormonal intervention does not therapeutically address the underlying psychological disorder. According to the American Foundation for Suicide Prevention (AFSP), 41% of self-identified, transgendered Americans have attempted to commit suicide; which is 25 times higher than the national average.

Moreover, since only a small minority of children who express gender-atypical thoughts or behaviour will continue to do so into adolescence or adulthood, such children should not be encouraged to become transgender, or to undertake surgery or hormone treatments. In fact, according to the American College of Pediatricians, the public promotion of transgenderism constitutes a form of child abuse, as indicated by the following:

> Conditioning children into believing that a lifetime of chemical and surgical impersonation of the opposite sex is normal and healthful is child abuse. Endorsing gender discordance as normal via public education and legal policies will confuse children and parents, leading more children to present [themselves] to 'gender clinics' where they will be given puberty-blocking drugs. This, in turn,

virtually ensures that they will 'choose' a lifetime of carcinogenic and otherwise toxic cross-sex hormones, and likely consider unnecessary surgical mutilation of their healthy body parts as young adults.

Disturbingly, yet predictably, the same irrational mental confusion that leads to gender identity disorder has also led to "racial identity disorder" (or racial dysphoria) and "species identity disorder" (or species dysphoria). "Transracialized" individuals don't identify with their inherited racial background; and instead, claim to belong to a different race—such as a white person claiming to be black; or a black person claiming to be white. And if that isn't mentally deranged enough, "transspecies" individuals don't regard themselves as human beings; but instead, identify as being non-human—such as an animal (otherwise known as "furries," "otherkins" or "therians"), an extraterrestrial, or even an inanimate object.

While transgenderism is a dysfunctional dissociation of body and self, according to esoteric science there is a transcendently-positive disengagement of body and self that can be achieved through initiatory training and development. Initiatory training truly begins with the conscious realization that the true-self of each human being is a reflection of the spirit of God. Sadly however, at this stage in evolution, most individuals are asleep to this fact. Consequently, a great deal of human behaviour continues to be subconsciously directed and influenced by deeply-rooted instinctual drives and impulses. For most individuals, then, the intrapsychic process of self-identification with one's physiological sex subconsciously occurs quite instinctively. In other words, most people today subconsciously connect their self-identity with their physical, sexual anatomy; thereby inwardly sensing: "I am a woman" or "I am a man."

Through initiatory development, the esoteric student learns that the spirit-self is immortal—existing before physical birth and after physical death. In other words, the human spirit-self can and does exist independently from the physical body. During physical life, the spirit-self karmically incarnates in a male or female body. Even though the spirit-self—as a true reflection of divine-spirit—transcends the biological distinctions of male and female, the trained initiate will consciously and deliberately choose to self-identify with his or her biological sex.

This consciously-chosen congruence of self and body on the part of the initiate is done to deliberately comply with the strict laws of karma. At this stage in human evolution, karmic law—which governs the conditions of destiny from one life to the next—determines whether it is beneficial for the spirit-self to be born as a man or a woman. Not complying with karmic law by self-identifying with the sex opposite to one's own—that is, by choosing to be transgender—is understood to result in serious and harmful conflicts of destiny; and is, therefore, never entertained by the advanced initiate.

6.4 Sexual Socialization versus Biological Sex

It is obvious, even to casual observation, that the expression of one's sexuality as male or female is greatly influenced by social conditioning and not genetically-determined biology. Some well-known examples are dressing male infants in blue and girl infants in pink; or men wearing pants and women wearing dresses; or men liking football and women liking ice-skating; or men working on cars and women knitting sweaters; or men reading repair manuals and women reading romance novels; or boys playing with superhero action-figures and girls playing with dolls. The list of examples could go on indefinitely; but the underlying point is that they all are variable behaviours, habits, social conventions and cultural expressions typically associated with each sex that are obviously not determined by genetics or biology.

Unfortunately over time, some of these socially-determined sexual expressions have become influential stereotypes that have been negatively used to restrict educational and occupational opportunities, particularly for women. For example, since the male physique is typically larger and stronger than the female form, men are more inclined to choose athletic professions, such as the military, law enforcement and firefighting. But this should not be a stereotypical barrier to talented and capable women (which it has been in the past). Likewise, due to a typically-powerful maternal instinct to care for and protect their children, women are more inclined to choose nurturing professions, such as nursing, elementary teaching and child-care workers. But again, men should not be stigmatized into rejecting these professions because of overly-restrictive stereotypes.

From an esoteric science perspective, men and women are equally capable, but to different degrees. For instance, though the fastest runners on earth are male Olympians, female athletes can definitely run fast as well. Though male Olympians hold the world records for weightlifting, female athletes can definitely lift heavy weights as well. Other than in the area of procreation, there is nothing that one sex can do, that the other sex can't do as well; though it may be to a different degree.

To fair and unbiased observation, then, male and female behaviour is clearly determined by both genetic biology *and* social conditioning. Unfortunately, radical gender theorists have gone to an intellectual extreme and irrationally postulated that one's sex as a man or a woman is *entirely* a social construct. Radical gender theorists entirely ignore and deliberately disregard the proven existence of binary sexual biology; that is, the physiological sex-differences in genetics, hormones, genitalia and reproductive anatomy.

Rather than blindly supporting such an irrational theory, political leftists, radical feminists and homosexual activists should be disturbed and threatened instead. If women are nothing but social constructs, why are radical-feminists agitating for increased women's rights? If male and female are simply social constructs, why do transgender persons want to change their sexual identity; why not mentally adjust their social construct instead of surgically altering their body? And for homosexual persons, why are they passionately attracted to the same sex when that sex is nothing but a social construct?

A theory of human sexuality, then, that deliberately ignores and rejects the existence of biological sex is logically out-of-touch with reality. To be seriously disconnected from reality in this way is delusional, and therefore psychotic. Radical gender theory, then, is a psychopathological notion that is soundly rejected by most religious denominations, political-conservatives and esoteric science.

6.5 Same-Sex Conjugal Union versus Sacramental Marriage

Just because homosexual persons express an anomalous sexual attraction to the same sex does not necessarily mean that they don't share many of the other deep-seated sexual and reproductive instincts that compel heterosexual persons. For example: the desire to have children, the desire to raise a family, the need for companionship, the desire for sexual intimacy, the desire for romance, the need to love and to be loved, and the desire to have a faithful and loving companion for life (that is, to be married).

As previously discussed in chapter sub-section 6.2, however, there are also those homosexual persons who rebelliously reject the idea of any affinity with heterosexual culture and lifestyle; and therefore strive to maintain a queer culture and lifestyle distinct from the mainstream. In other words, the compelling desire to be married is not necessarily shared by all homosexual persons.

According to esoteric science, the reason why the marital urge is so strong, so cross-cultural and so universal is because marriage is not just a socially-established convention; but rather a divinely-inspired instinct, subconsciously implanted by celestial beings for the good of the spouses, the good of the children, the good of society and the good of human evolution on earth. Moreover, the divine intention (the spiritual ideal) of marriage is to reflect the familial love of the divine Trinity; that is, the eternal and infinite love between the Heavenly Father, the Holy Mother and the Eternal Son.

Not surprisingly, mankind throughout history has fallen short of even partially realizing such a transcendent ideal for marriage. Nevertheless, many world religions such as Judaism, Christianity, Hinduism and Sikhism recognize marriage as a sacred duty or institution.

Unfortunately, due to the cumulative effects of sin, sickness, evil and death, mankind during the Graeco-Roman cultural era was critically falling away from its entire divinely-intended evolutionary-path on earth. Hence, the salvational incarnation of Christ-Jesus in order to effectively arrest and reverse humanity's fallen condition. By uniting his own divinely-infused life with earth evolution, Christ-Jesus provided the supernatural power (or "grace") necessary to realize mankind's spiritual destiny.

In the case of marriage, by uniting his own life with the conjugal union of husband and wife, Christ-Jesus raises it from being a "covenant" (a contract between God and mankind), to being a "sacrament" (a physical event permeated with his supernatural grace)—the "sacrament of holy matrimony." As succinctly expressed in the *Catechism of the Catholic Church*:

The matrimonial covenant, by which a man and a woman establish between themselves a partnership of the whole of life, is by its nature ordered toward the good of the spouses and the procreation and education of offspring; this covenant between baptized persons has been raised by Christ the Lord to the dignity of a sacrament.

Obviously a same-sex conjugal union can never be a sacramental marriage since it is lacking one fundamental requirement: the union must be between a man and a woman in order to unite the procreative complementarity of male and female that has its origin in the transcendent perfection of the divine Trinity.[37]

Since there exists a spiritual archetype (model) of the ideal marriage, same-sex unions will very often attempt to duplicate (usually unknowingly) that model. For instance, in order to approximate the marital complementarity of opposite sexes, same-sex couples will often assume typical male and female roles: one partner will assume responsibility for the household repairs, car maintenance and landscaping chores that men often do; while the other partner will assume responsibility for cooking, shopping and household decorating that women often do. As well, since same-sex couples are biologically unable to procreate, if they wish to comply with the typical marital model of having children and raising a family, then they're forced to adopt, to employ a surrogate birth-mother or to use artificial insemination.

Many traditionalists, political conservatives and religious denominations (particularly the Catholic Church) oppose the use of the word "marriage" in connection with same-sex unions. If marriage is strictly defined as "the conjugal union of a man and a woman," then this doesn't logically apply to same-sex unions. Linguistically, however, the word "marriage" can be used in a variety of ways; such as "a marriage of ideas"; or "a marriage of blues and gospel music." In this broader sense of the word, there are a number of different kinds of marriage; for example: (1) a traditional marriage, (2) a heterosexual marriage, (3) a monogamous marriage, (4) a polygamous marriage, (5) an arranged marriage, (6) a sacramental marriage, (7) a common-law marriage and (8) a same-sex marriage.

Unfortunately in today's increasingly secular, materialistic and permissive society—fewer and fewer couples (whether same-sex or opposite-sex) are choosing to marry. In Europe, for example, the number of marriages decreased by 30% from 1975 to 2005. As for those in Western society who still choose to marry, a disturbingly large percentage unhappily end in divorce. In 2008, about 45% of marriages in Britain ended in divorce. Similarly in the US, a 2011 census report indicated that about 46% of American marriages ended in divorce.

From an esoteric science point of view, the widespread abnegation of marriage and the high rate of divorce is cause for concern. Since the spirits of darkness use every opportunity to further their own nefarious agenda for mankind, by encouraging the increased rejection of marriage, they intend to destabilize healthy human society by eroding one of its foundational supports—the strong and vibrant traditional family.

6.6 The Immoral Practice of Abortion

It is obvious to any spiritually-minded person, that humanity is in a deep moral crisis when mothers feel justified in killing their own unborn children in the name of "reproductive rights"; and governments around the world are willing to make it legal and medically accessible to do so.

Abortion is the logical consequence of irrationally accepting the faulty notion that there is no purpose to human sexuality. If procreation for human survivability is not one of the prime purposes of human sexuality, then pregnancy can be negatively regarded as an undesirable side-effect of sexual freedom. If pregnancy cannot be contraceptively eliminated from sexual activity, then abortion is the perfect medical solution.

All arguments that justify or rationalize the intentional killing of an unborn child, except perhaps when the life of the mother is threatened, are specious at best and diabolical at worst. Take for instance, the silly argument that abortion is a routine surgical procedure since the fetus is not a human life, but simply a clump of cells. In other words, an abortion is no different than removing an unwanted polyp or tumorous growth.

The fault of this argument?—it's logically, medically and scientifically absurd to claim that a fetus is not a human life. Of course it's a human life. From the moment of conception, the fetus has the unique, individualized genetic profile of a human being. The fetus will not develop into a carrot or a canary. It is human; and in order to biologically self-develop in utero, it must obviously be alive.

A cleverer (but equally spurious) extension of this argument acknowledges that the fetus is a "human life," but claims that it is not a "human person." Therefore, the fetus has no legal rights, including a right to life. Accordingly, while abortion does deliberately terminate a human life, it cannot be legally regarded as homicide or murder; and is thereby morally acceptable.

According to this argument, a fetus only becomes a person with legal rights when it is "born"; that is, when it is outside the mother's womb and the umbilical cord is severed. In this case, the prime determinant of personhood is whether or not the fetus can survive outside the uterus, and without umbilical attachment to the mother's body. The term that is used to describe independent fetal survival ex utero is "viability." In other words, a fetus becomes a person when it is viable.[38]

The problem is, however, that even after being successfully delivered, a newborn infant cannot in any way survive on its own. In many critical ways, a newborn is just as dependent for food, protection and health-care as a late-term fetus; yet the fetus is not considered a person (or even a human being); but an equally-dependent newborn is.

Moreover, this argument fails to acknowledge that human life is constantly going through various stages of development: fetalhood, infanthood, childhood, teenagehood, adulthood, middle-age and seniorhood. Just being at an early stage of development does not mean that one is any less of a human being. In other words, just because a child is not an adult does not mean that the child is not a human person deserving of legal rights. Likewise, just because an unborn child is not a newborn child does not disqualify the fetal child from being recognized as a developing human being—as a "person in development"

And what is even more legally twisted and absurd in today's materialistic culture is that while an unborn child is denied legal status as a person, business corporations can legally register as persons. As explained by Joel Bakan in *The Corporation: The Pathological Pursuit of Profit and Power* (2005):

> By the end of the nineteenth century, through a bizarre legal alchemy, courts had fully transformed the corporation into a "person," with its own identity, separate from the flesh-and-blood people who were its owners and managers and empowered, like a real person, to conduct business in its own name, acquire assets, employ workers, pay taxes, and go to court to assert its rights and defend its actions. The corporate person had taken the place, at least in law, of the real people who owned corporations. Now viewed as an entity, "not imaginary or fictitious, but real, not artificial but natural," as it was described by one law professor in 1911, the corporation had been reconceived as a free and

independent being.

Another oft-heard but bogus argument—used particularly by radical-feminists to rationalize abortion—passionately alleges that "abortion is a woman's reproductive right." More specifically, the argument alleges that since pregnancy pertains to a woman's body, governments have no authority to tell a woman what she can and cannot do with her own body. Considering how logically flawed this argument is, it's astounding how often it is used by government agencies around the world to promote abortion.

The fact is, governments everywhere legally restrict what women can and can't do with their bodies in a number of familiar ways. For example, in many countries it is against the law for women to sell their bodies for sex. Women are not allowed to appear nude in shopping malls. It is illegal for women to have sex with minors. In many countries, it is illegal for women to inject their bodies with heroin. In many Moslem countries, women are not allowed to appear in public without being covered by a burqa. It is still illegal in many countries for depressed women to kill themselves with the assistance of a physician.

While this list of examples could go on and on, it is more than sufficient to demonstrate that women do not have unfettered use of their own bodies in the eyes of the law. Moreover, the "right to life" is supposed to be a fundamental and universal right in a civilized society. As such, this right must also apply to an unborn child; and thereby supersede any "reproductive right" to abortion.

One further argument commonly used to justify abortion is that even if abortion is once again declared to be illegal (as it was in the past), women will continue to seek out underground, "black-market" abortionists (as they did in the past). Continuing to provide legal abortions, then, is a necessary social evil that will prevent desperate women from being harmed or killed by non-professional, back-alley butchers; or from harming themselves with dangerous drugs or unsafe uterine insertions.

While this argument is indeed a disturbing reminder of the horrible abortion practices of the past, social conditions are much improved today; and therefore, there are much better alternatives available for unwanted pregnancies. Moreover, delivering a child outside of marriage does not necessarily condemn the single mother to a life of poverty, as it did in the past. Currently as well, there is little social stigmatization of extramarital pregnancy, and there are far more social agencies that can provide prenatal advice and assistance. Besides, the easiest solution to an unwanted pregnancy is not to abort the innocent unborn child; but instead, to put the newborn child up for adoption. The sad irony of Western society today is that while numerous women are procuring abortions, there are an equal number of childless couples who are desperately seeking to adopt a child.[39]

Worldwide, the number of induced abortions is staggering. According to the World Health Organization, every year there are an estimated 40–50 million abortions performed (which is about 125,000 abortions per day). In the US alone, there are over 3,000 abortions per day. Disturbingly, nearly half of American pregnancies are unintended; with 4 out of 10 being terminated by abortion.

So, what does esoteric science have to say regarding these disturbing statistics? Well, from an esoteric science point of view, abortion is a serious spiritual concern. Not only does it negatively interfere with the karmic necessity of incoming souls to incarnate under the best possible circumstances; but it is also being encouraged by the spirits of darkness in order to restrict and thwart the divinely-intended mission of human evolution. In fact, there is even a particular demonic being, esoterically known as "Lilith," whose evil occupation within the "twelve demi-lords of hell" is the promotion of debauchery and abortion.[40]

Unfortunately for the spirits of darkness, even though the widescale aborting of unborn children has a brutalizing, dehumanizing and corrupting effect on world-society, this genocidal martyrdom of innocent, unborn children has correspondingly released an army of vestigial souls with vast reserves of latent spiritual force into the etheric realm closest to the earth. This collective torrent of supersensible light works to resist Ahrimanic materialism in the etheric realm, and to spiritually protect other incoming souls preparing for earthly incarnation.

6.7 The Mainstreaming of Sexual Deviations and Perversions

Once human sexuality is intellectually and socially stripped of its true, divinely-intended purpose—that is, for the complementary union of husband and wife, and for the healthy procreation and education of children—then it can very easily degenerate into simply becoming a hedonistic, self-indulgent sensual pleasure. When hedonistic pleasure without moral consideration becomes the exclusive focus of sexual activity, then it's not long before the prime behavioural directive becomes "anything goes."

Such is the case today in the continuing aftermath of the sexual revolution. What were once considered "sexual perversions" and "sexual deviations" are now medically euphemized into "paraphilias." Some paraphilia examples are: sexual sadism and masochism (S & M); transvestism, sexual fetishism, bondage and discipline (B & D), dominance and submission (D & S), bestiality (zoophilia), exhibitionism, pedophilia, pederasty, necrophilia, rape, and voyeurism.

Increasingly, many of these paraphilic disorders are being medically regarded as "normal variants of sexual interest." Such phraseology is simply deceptive medical double-speak.

A "variant" from normal "sexual interest" is by definition an "abnormal deviation." By engaging in such deceptive language in order to promote the widespread enabling of psychological disorders, irresponsible medical professionals are fashioning an unhealthy, dissolute and dysfunctional society.

Rather than therapeutically treating the deviant disorder, today's psychologists, psychiatrists and psychotherapists are only interested in treating the "dysphoria"—any negative feelings such as guilt, shame or embarrassment associated with the disorder. The goal of therapy is to learn to accept the deviant disorder as "normal."

For those already uncomfortable with the outdoor spectacle of a pride parade, it will come as a huge shock that since 1984 there has been an annual, weeklong, late-September event in San Francisco, called the Folsom Street Fair, that publicly celebrates "kink culture"; that is, sexual deviance and fetishism—particularly BDSM (bondage, domination, sadism and masochism). The event is currently attended by about 400,000 participants and spectators.

But perhaps the best indication that sexual perversion has become mainstream in America is that the Fair has received corporate support from Marriott Marquis Hotel (owned by the Mormons) and American Airlines, among many others. Moreover, the Fair organization is considered a non-profit charity, and donates the money raised at the event.

And the Folsom Street Fair is not alone. There are many more such events for heterosexuals as well as homosexuals, such as the Hedofest in Washington, Texas; Life Style West in Las Vegas; the Key West Fantasy Fest; the International Leatherman in Chicago; and the Mid-Atlantic Leather Association in Washington, DC. For many Americans today, then—especially millennials—fetishes and kinky deviations have been seductively integrated into their lifestyle culture.

So, other than widespread exposure and proliferation

through internet pornography, what accounts for the current increase in sexual fetishism, perversion and deviance. The primary explanation has to do with the underlying nature of sexual reproductive energy (libido) itself. Sexual energy is a powerful, creative life-force that innately seeks physical expression. If it isn't properly channeled within the healthy confines of marriage between husband and wife, then sexual life-energy will "deviate" into any number of estranged channels of physical expression; hence the term, "sexual deviation." Moreover, keeping sexual life-energy physically constrained, or "repressed," for any length of time will only cause internal physiological and psychological disturbance, disruption and disorder.

Fortunately, if there is no appropriate opportunity for the conjugal expression of sexual energy, since it is a creative life-force by nature, it can be positively channeled or "sublimated" into other healthy creative outlets and expressions; such as painting, sculpture, music, sport, landscaping, cooking, sewing, writing, pottery and so on.

Practitioners of tantric yoga also attempt to consciously channel sexual energy; in this case, in order to achieve spiritual enlightenment. While properly-sublimated creative life-force can certainly contribute to a healthy mind and body, most Western practitioners of tantric yoga are simply pleasure-seeking dilettantes looking to orgasmically enhance their sex life.

While much of the sexual perversion and deviation that is being mainstreamed in Western societies today certainly constitutes a de-humanizing debauchery that corrupts individual lives and society-at-large, there is an even more insidious and evil manifestation known as "sex magick." In this case, the reproductive life-force is debased and corrupted; then used in black magic rituals to awaken dark occult powers and knowledge.

Very often these depraved rituals will involve the torture

and mutilation of animals and human victims; and on occasion, ritual sacrifice and murder. Fortunately the number of serious black magicians is few; unfortunately their power and influence is disproportionate to their numbers. All black magicians eventually come under the control of Sorath, the sun-demon (known biblically as the "two-horned beast that rises up out of the abyss").

CONCLUSION

AS VIEWED BY esoteric science, the present-day confusion in the once-immutable area of human gender and sexuality is a symptom of a much larger spiritual struggle occurring in our time. The sexual revolution is one of many ideological and sociological skirmishes that are being fought by the spirits of darkness against the spirits of light—with the fate of humanity depending on the outcome.

As indicated by the anthroposophical research of Rudolf Steiner, the age of darkness (known as "kali yuga" in Hindu philosophy) that began in 3101 BC, came to an end in 1899. As well, the age of Michael (a period of world evolution under the guidance and inspiration of St. Michael the archai) began in 1879, and will continue for the next 354 years. In other words, humanity has recently entered a golden age of light; during which intellectual access to the spiritual world is readily accessible to every sincere seeker, and not just high initiates.

Unfortunately, an "age of deception" has also been simultaneously established by the spirits of darkness to counteract the recently-begun age of light; as well as to prepare for the earthly incarnation of Ahriman, which is destined to occur sometime during the next thousand years.

Throughout history, Ahriman (also known as Satan, Mephistopheles, the Devil or the Great Red Dragon) has been referred to as "the father of lies." This is because he purposely distorts physical sensory perception, and deliberately blocks any human perception of the spiritual world. By doing so, Ahriman (and his superphysical cohorts) foster the big lie that the physical world is the only reality that exists, that God and the spiritual world have no existence, and that human beings are nothing more than sophisticated animals.

Consequently, the spiritual conflict taking place today is a renewed battle of Michael (the advanced archangel) and the Dragon (Satan-Ahriman); only in this case, it is not a "war in heaven"—but one that is taking place on earth. As a worldwide result, individual human beings and societies in general are becoming increasingly polarized between those that (consciously or unconsciously) follow the spiritual direction of St. Michael, and those that follow the materialistic direction of Ahriman.

Ideologically, this raging supernatural battle on earth has engendered two competing world-views: one fostered by St. Michael and the spirits of light; and the other fostered by Ahriman and the spirits of darkness.

The worldview promoted by St. Michael envisions a peaceful, international association of freely-democratic sovereign states where governments are inspired by a shared love of God and a love for all mankind. Within individual societies, there is a healthy autonomy and cooperation amongst the three social spheres: (1) economic (business, trade), (2) political (law-courts, police, military) and (3) cultural (science, education, arts, religion, media). Thereby, freedom of religion without undue political or economic interference is guaranteed.

While governance is decided by a well-informed and morally-advanced majority, minority groups are ensured a political voice, and are treated fairly and justly. Atypical and non-normative differences are not cause for discrimination, stigmatization or marginalization; but are treated with understanding and compassion. Those individuals suffering from mental, emotional and physical disorders, however, are not pseudo-empathically enabled; but are provided truly-beneficial medical care. The right to human life is respected from conception until natural death.

The opposing worldview promoted by Ahriman envisions a one-world government (known as the "new world order") that is entirely controlled by a financial elite. The rest of humanity function as unwitting servants who are kept obedient and compliant through indoctrination institutions, media propaganda and medical interventions (such as drugs and surgery). Individual nation states are controlled by subordinates of the global elite; who subserviently wield the governing power of the socialist state to maintain public order and to keep the population docile and submissive.

Any religious groups that manage to temporarily survive are deliberately marginalized and rendered ineffectual in any governing decisions (since religious freedom is in no way guaranteed). Since human beings are collectively regarded as sophisticated animals, all manner of sexual deviance and perversion is enabled and permitted, so long as their practice doesn't unduly upset the social order. Abortion, contrived epidemics, sectarian violence and local wars are all occasionally orchestrated by the global elite for population control.

Not surprisingly, those individuals and groups that are siding (either consciously or unconsciously) with the spiritual forces of St. Michael are Judeo-Christian religious groups and moderate political-conservatives. Those individuals and groups that are siding (almost all being hypnotically unaware) with the atheistic, materialistic forces of Satan-Ahriman are anti-Christian religious groups and fanatical political-socialists.

It's important to understand that the Ahrimanic worldview is a deceptive lie and a deliberate distortion of true reality. As such, it creates a false, substitute reality in the minds of human beings. Being disconnected from reality is, unfortunately, a seriously delusion; and is therefore a psychopathological condition. Disturbingly, in the eyes of those who cling to the truth, much of what is being said, done and advanced by radical political-socialists throughout Western society is a form of group insanity.

In light of esoteric science, the most effective and powerful method of maintaining spiritual truth and resisting spiritual deception, falsehood and lies is to unite with the embodied spirit of truth—Christ-Jesus. Since the incarnation of Christ-Jesus two thousand years ago, spiritual truth is no longer just a transcendent ideal; it is now embodied in an actual person. This is the literal meaning of our Saviour's well-known self-identifier: "I AM the way, and *the truth*, and the life" (Jn 14:6).

By uniting with the spiritual truth embodied in Christ-Jesus, one is afforded supernatural protection from evil and the intellectual discernment to see through and resist the delusion of Darwinian evolution, the delusion of atomic theory, the delusion of atheism, the delusion of materialism, the delusion of radical socialism, the delusion of multiple genders and the delusion of transgender theory.

NOTES

INTRODUCTION

1. The term, "esoteric science" is here used in a broad, general sense to include the various spiritual and mystical disciplines throughout history that have sincerely and seriously searched for the deeper truths of life and existence. Some examples are Yoga philosophy, Egyptian Hermeticism, Jewish Kabbalism, Greek mystery-wisdom, Holy Grail mythology, Rosicrucian teaching and modern-day anthroposophical literature.

2. "Luciferic beings" refers mainly to a class of undeveloped angels who did not complete their required evolution in the distant past. Consequently, they exist at a stage midway between angels and humanity. Since these demi-angels are out-of-step with current, progressive evolution, their interference in human development has mostly been inimical and regressive. They take their group-designation from their more powerful leader, the retrograde spirit of wisdom popularly known as "Lucifer."

   "Ahrimanic beings" refers mainly to a class of retrograde archangels, who take their group-designation from their heinous leader, "Ahriman," a fallen-away power or spirit of form. Throughout history, Ahriman has also been known as Satan, Mephistopheles, the Devil and the Great Red Dragon. The Ahrimanic beings continually strive to compress spiritual substance into physical matter. Moreover, they are hostile and opposed to rightful human evolution on earth.

CHAPTER 1

3. The "Big Bang" theory of cosmic origin was first proposed in 1927 by Catholic priest, astronomer and physicist, George Lemaitre (1894–1966). Lemaitre originally referred to the cosmic singularity as the "primeval atom" or the "cosmic egg."

4. Unfamiliar to most non-scientists, the modern concept of "Einsteinian space" or "physical space" is quite different than the older, more familiar concept of "Newtonian space." Newtonian space was long considered to be an absolute condition of emptiness that was devoid of any physical properties. Einsteinian space, however, can be affected by matter; as well as curved and bent by gravitational fields.

   Regarding the hypothetical "luminiferous or light ether" and "physical space," theoretical physicist George Gamow (1904–1968) has stated:

   > [S]pace may possess certain morphological or structural features that make it a much more complicated thing than it is in the conceptions of Euclidean geometry [or Newtonian space]. In fact, in modern physics the expressions "light ether" (divested of its alleged mechanical properties) and "physical space" are considered synonymous. (*One Two Three ... Infinity*; 1972)

CHAPTER 2

5. There are of course, certain developmental stages, mental states, and physical injuries where individuals do not appear to exhibit "waking-state" self-awareness; but that does not necessarily mean they are no longer regarded as "persons." In cases where an individual is comatose from an accident, or is suffering from late-stage Alzheimer's disease, or is a very young infant, or maybe just in a state of deep sleep—self-awareness is not fully exhibited because the ego-bearing soul and astral body are semi-detached from the physical body. Nevertheless, the fact that these particular individuals still retain an ego-self and a consciousness-vehicle attached to their physical body means that they are still esoterically acknowledged to be human "persons."

6. Esoteric science and Western theology both recognize a celestial hierarchy comprised of nine levels of advanced, superphysical beings: (1) angels, (2) archangels, (3) principalities, (4) powers, (5) virtues, (6) dominions, (7) thrones, (8) cherubim and (9) seraphim.

7. The designation, "Eternal Son," has been esoterically chosen to conform with Christ-Jesus' biblical reference to the Trinity as "Father, Son and Holy Spirit" (Matt 28:19). Nevertheless, it's important to understand that the designation is not meant to imply that the divine Son is an additional masculine personification of God's spirit-nature. Instead, the Eternal Son is esoterically understood to be the perfect union of divine masculinity (the Heavenly Father) *and* divine femininity (the Holy Mother). For this reason, the Eternal Son is also occasionally referred to as the "divine Offspring" or the "divine Progeny."

8. In the early years of Christianity, it was not uncommon to refer to the Holy Spirit as the "Holy Mother" or the

"divine Sophia." For example, St. Jerome (347–420), the translator of the Latin Vulgate wrote:

> In the Gospel of the Hebrews that the Nazarenes read it says, "Just now my mother, the Holy Spirit, took me." Now no one should be offended by this, because 'spirit' in Hebrew is feminine, while in our [Latin] language it is masculine and in the Greek it is neuter. (*Jerome's Commentary on Isaiah II*)

Moreover, second-century Church leader, Clement of Alexandria (c.150–c.215), wrote:

> And God Himself is love; and out of love to us became feminine. In His ineffable essence He is Father; in His compassion to us He became Mother. The Father by loving became feminine: and the great proof of this is He whom He begot of Himself [the Son]: and the fruit brought forth by love is love. (*Who is the Rich Man that Shall be Saved*; Chap. 37)

9. St. John Paul II in a General Audience (November 20, 1985) concisely explained the Catholic Church's position on Trinitarian "genesis":

> The Father who begets loves the Son who is begotten. The Son loves the Father with a love which is identical with that of the Father. In the unity of the divinity, love is on one side paternal and on the other, filial. At the same time the Father and the Son are not only united by that mutual love as two Persons infinitely perfect. But their mutual gratification, their reciprocal love, proceeds in them and from them as a person. The Father and the Son "spirate" the Spirit of Love consubstantially with them. In this way God, in the absolute unity of the divinity, is from all eternity Father, Son and Holy Spirit.

10. As biblically stated:

> Beloved, let us love one another; for love is of God, and he who loves is born of God and knows God. He who does not love does not know God; for God is love. (1 John 4:7, 8)

11. For a much deeper and more comprehensive esoteric study of the Divine Trinity, the interested reader is referred to this authour's previous publication, entitled: *The Greater Mysteries of the Divine Trinity, the Logos-Word and Creation* (2015); available from Amazon.com.

CHAPTER 3

12. Another popular rationale for replacing the word "sex" with "gender" is because "sex" has become a widely-used shortened expression for "sexual intercourse" or "sexual activity"; rather than an exclusive term for male or female.

13. This of course especially applies to the spirit-nature of God. While perfect personifications of masculine and feminine gender are an eternally-essential aspect of God's spirit-nature, the terms "male" and "female" cannot be correctly applied at the divine level since there is no necessary sexual differentiation.

14. Interestingly, the word "sperm" comes from the Greek word "sperma" which means "seed."

15. In Judeo-Christian theology, the understanding that human sexuality—the existence of two sexes: male and female—has a divine origin is biblically conveyed in Genesis: "So God created man in his own image, in the image of God he created him; male and female he created them" (Gen 1:27).

16. Catholic theology also clearly and vigorously asserts that

there is a divine purpose to human sexuality. As stated in the *Catechism of the Catholic Church* (paragraph 2360–2362):

> Sexuality is ordered to the conjugal love between a man and a woman ... by means of which man and woman give themselves to one another through the acts which are proper and exclusive to spouses, is not something simply biological, but concerns the innermost being of the human person as such. It is realized in a truly human way only if it is an integral part of the love by which a man and woman commit themselves totally to one another until death. ... The Creator himself ... established that in the [generative] function, spouses should experience pleasure and enjoyment of body and spirit.

17. According to anthroposophical spiritual science, our present-day solar system—including planet earth—has undergone a rhythmic series of smaller-scale, Big Bang-style expansions and collapses. There have been three such occurrences in the primordial past; esoterically termed (1) the "Ancient Saturn Period" of planetary development, (2) the "Ancient Sun Period" of planetary development and (3) the "Ancient Moon Period" of planetary development. Our current solar system is termed the "Present Earth Period" of planetary development.

    Moreover, in accordance with the divinely-formulated evolutionary plan for planet earth, there will be three additional stages in the future; esoterically termed: (1) the "Future Jupiter Period," (2) the "Future Venus Period," and (3) the "Future Vulcan Period."

18. As biblically conveyed:

> But from the beginning of creation, 'God made them male and female.' 'For this reason a man shall leave his father and mother and be joined to his wife, and

the two shall become one.' (Mk 10:6–8)

As conveyed in the *Catechism of the Catholic Church* (paragraph 372):

> Man and woman were made "for each other"—not that God left them half-made and incomplete: he created them to be a communion of persons, in which each can be "helpmate" to the other, for they are equal as persons ... and complementary as masculine and feminine. In marriage God unites them in such a way that, by forming "one flesh," they can transmit human life ... By transmitting human life to their descendants, man and woman as spouses and parents co-operate in a unique way in the Creator's work.

19. This of course also applies to God. Existing entirely as pure spirit, the divine nature certainly transcends any human sexual distinctions of male or female. Nevertheless, male and female sexuality have their supernal origin in the divine gender personifications of the Heavenly Father and the Holy Mother. This important understanding is also echoed in basic Christian theology:

> In no way is God in man's image. He is neither man nor woman. God is pure spirit in which there is no place for the difference between the sexes. But the respective "perfections" of man and woman reflect something of the infinite perfection of God: those of a mother and those of a father and husband. (paragraph 370; *Catechism of the Catholic Church*)

CHAPTER 4

20. In a lecture given on 25 October 1905, Rudolf Steiner has similarly stated:

> A second severance followed. With the Moon everything connected with self-reproduction departed from the Earth ... Then the possibility of self-fertilization ceased; the Moon had drawn out what made this possible. Then the Moon was outside and there were beings who were no longer able to reproduce themselves; thus in the Lemurian Age the two sexes originated.
>
> The leader of this whole progression is the God who in the Hebraic tradition is called Jahve; Jehovah. He was a Moon-God. He possessed in the highest sense of the word, the power that had developed on the [Ancient] Moon [period of planetary development] and accordingly he endeavoured to develop mankind further in this direction. In the earthly world Jahve represents that God who endows beings with the possibility of physical reproduction. (Published in *Foundations of Esotericism*; 1983)

21. Just as the loss of the power of self-fertilization and the consequent separation of the sexes was connected with the extrusion of the moon during the Lemurian Age, so is the future regaining of the power of self-fertilization through the reunion of sexual forces connected with the re-incorporation of the moon during the eighth millennium. As conveyed by Rudolf Steiner in a lecture given in Dornach on 13 May 1921, and entitled "Materialism/Anthroposophy":

> Now you know that one day the moon will reunite with the earth ... In reality, we are not so very far away from that point in time ... [I]n the seventh millennium, a time will come ... Then, women will

cease to be fertile; an entirely different form of living on earth will come about. That will be the time when the moon will again approach the earth and will be incorporated into it ...

[I]t is intended that the human being shall be lifted up, in that time when women will no longer be fertile, when the eighth millennium will have arrived and the moon will unite again with the earth ...

At the time of the departure of the moon, physical birth commenced. The human being began to be born of woman. Just as this came to pass, so in the future the human being will no longer be born of woman. For that is only a passing episode in the whole of cosmic evolution. (Published in *Materialism and the Task of Anthroposophy*; 1987)

22. As indicated by Rudolf Steiner in a lecture given on 12 April 1917:

[S]piritual investigation shows that in the sixth and seventh millennium there will be a decline in fertility. Women will become increasingly sterile. The present method of reproduction will no longer be possible; it must be transposed to a higher plane. (Published in *Building Stones for an Understanding of the Mystery of Golgotha*; 1985)

23. The clairvoyant knowledge concerning the future reproductive function of the larynx has been faithfully guarded within the hidden Rosicrucian Order, whose teachings visualized the Holy Grail chalice as a mystical symbol of the Christ-transformed larynx of the future.

CHAPTER 5

24. In esoteric science, Canada, the United States and Australia are still regarded as colonial off-shoots of Anglo-European culture; and not entirely independent cultures of their own.

25. The viewpoint that there is no objective standard of right and wrong, and that morality is entirely subject to time and place is known as "moral relativism."

26. Child pornography is still regarded as an illegal sexual taboo in Western society, even though there is a growing movement in Western academia to legitimize sexual activity between adults and children. Moreover, there are advocacy groups in most Western countries that promote pedophilia and pederasty as the next "sexual rights" revolution.

    Even bestiality (or "zoophilia") is no longer illegal in some Western countries. In Germany, for example, "bestiality brothels" and "erotic zoos" are increasingly being established to facilitate sexual activity with animals as a "lifestyle choice." As for Denmark, it has become known as a "hot spot" for the animal sex-tourism industry. Hungary (where bestiality and animal brothels are also legal) is currently one of the three largest producers of bestiality x-rated films in the world (the other two countries are Brazil and Japan).

    Even in many states in America, bestiality is not illegal; states such as Nevada, New Hampshire, New Mexico, Ohio, Texas, Vermont, West Virginia and Wyoming. And of course south of the border in Mexico, where "donkey shows"—a lewd entertainment spectacle where a woman has sexual relations with a donkey—is a popular tourist offering.

27. As expressed by Rudolf Steiner in a lecture given on 04 June 1908, and later published in *The Influence of Spiritual Beings Upon Man* (1982):

    We have pointed out that in the man of the last third

of the Atlantean age, before the Atlantean flood, the relation of etheric body to physical body was quite different from what it had been earlier. Today the physical part of the head and the etheric part practically coincide. That was quite different in ancient Atlantis; there we have the etheric part of the head projecting far out—especially in the region of the forehead. We now have a central point for the etheric and physical parts approximately between the eyebrows. These two parts came together in the last third of the Atlantean age and today they coincide. Thereby man is able to say "I" to himself and feel an independent personality. Thus the etheric and physical bodies of the head have joined together. This has come about so that man could become the sense being that he is within our physical world …

28. In a lecture given on 01 May 1919, entitled "Esoteric Prelude to an Exoteric Consideration of the Social Question I," Rudolf Steiner stated the following:

[A]s soon as we cross the threshold into the supersense world … then there takes place in our soul an absolute separation of thinking, feeling, and willing.

We are living in the fifth post-Atlantean period; and in this period mankind must go through in its evolution as a whole something similar to what the crossing of the threshold into the supersense world is for an individual. Mankind as a whole, I said, in its cosmic—or we can say if we like terrestrial—evolution, is crossing a threshold …

For the crossing of this threshold must truly not remain in the unconscious. Men must become aware of it, otherwise they will sleep right through, or at least dream right through, an event that is very important for them.

29. As stated by Rudolf Steiner in a lecture given on 08 November 1906, entitled "The Origin of Suffering," and later published in *Supersensible Knowledge* (1987):

> There are three soul forces in human beings: thinking, feeling and willing. These three forces are bound up with the physical organization ...
>
> In the normally constituted human being of today, thinking, feeling and willing are in harmony. This is right at certain stages of evolution. However, it must be born in mind that as far as a person is concerned, this harmony is established unconsciously. If a person is to be initiated, if he or she is to become capable of higher perception, then thinking, feeling and willing must be severed from one another. The organs connected with feeling and will must undergo division ... should [a division] occur without a higher consciousness being attained, insanity would set in. Insanity is in fact a condition in which the three soul members have separated without being ruled by a higher consciousness.

30. A great deal of specific and detailed information on this significant but often overlooked occurrence (even amongst informed esotericists) was provided by Rudolf Steiner in a lecture given on 26 October 1917 entitled "The Spirits of Light and the Spirits of Darkness":

> [F]rom the last third of the nineteenth century the situation has been completely reversed. The spirits of light ... have done enough where the establishment of blood, tribal, racial and similar bonds is concerned, for everything has its time in evolution ... In more recent times, therefore, the spirits of light have

changed their function. They now inspire human beings to develop independent ideas, feelings and impulses for freedom; they now make it their concern to establish the basis on which people can be independent individuals. And it is gradually becoming the task of the spirits who are related to the old spirits of darkness to work within the blood bonds.

The function which was right in the past or, better said, belonged to the sphere of the good spirits of light, was handed over to the spirits of darkness during the last third of the nineteenth century. From this time onwards, the old impulses based on racial, tribal and national relationships, on the blood, became the domain of the spirits of darkness, who had previously been rebels in the cause of independence. They then began to instill ideas in human minds that affairs should be ordered on the basis of tribal relationships, of blood bonds. (Published in *The Fall of the Spirits of Darkness*, 1993)

CHAPTER 6

31. According to the estimates of the Intersex Society of North America, intersex births are less than 0.01%—about 1 in 1500 to about 1 in 2000.

32. Obviously homosexuality in small numbers is no threat to human survivability; only that, in general, exclusive sexual relations with the same sex is not biologically capable of procreation.

33. Current scientific research and clinical literature generally regard homosexuality as a "normal variation of human sexuality." This is actually a clever but specious way of describing homosexuality as "normal" when it statistically is not. What the phrase is actually saying is that

homosexuality is a "normal departure from the norm of human sexuality (that is, heterosexuality)." A departure (or variation) from the norm by definition makes it "abnormal" or "non-normative." What this illogical phrase is saying, then, is that homosexuality is a "normal abnormality"—a clear contradiction in terms. This is like saying that cancer is a normal variation of good health.

34. A US census in 2010 indicated that 80% of the children being raised by American same-sex couples were not adopted, and that most were the result of previous heterosexual marriages. This obviously shows that at least one of these same-sex parents changed their sexual orientation.

35. "Political-socialism" is a pernicious ideology that currently defines the political left throughout Western democracies. It is loosely based on atheistic, Marxist philosophy that contends that society is exclusively shaped by economic forces; particularly the struggle between the rich and the poor, between the wealthy capitalist few and the underprivileged, working-class many. Moreover, the wealthy are the victimizing oppressors, and the working poor are the oppressed victims.

While anti-poverty and union activists wholly subscribe to this basic, Marxist interpretation of society, various other identity-groups claiming to be "victimized minorities" have altered the basic socialist model to fit their own particular narrative. For instance, radical-feminists claim that women are the oppressed victims in society, and that men are the victimizing oppressors. Black and Hispanic activists in the US claim that wealthy white-Americans are the victimizing oppressors, and that poor black-Americans and Hispanic-Americans are the oppressed victims. Radical Islamists claim that Christianity is the victimizing oppressor, and that Moslem culture is the oppressed victim. Aboriginal activists claim that European colonists are the victimizing oppressors, and that marginalized aboriginals are the oppressed victims. Homosexual activists claim that heterosexuals are the victimizing oppressors, and that homosexuals are the oppressed victims.

All these victimized minorities agree that wealthy, white, heterosexual Christian men are the primary, victimizing oppressors in Western society. Therefore, the radical, alt-left political activists feel justified in labeling them "misogynist, homophobic, racist, Islamophobic, xenophobic, bigoted white-supremacists." Disturbingly as well, the Marxist solution to societal oppression is revolution, the radical political overthrow of those in power, and their replacement with a socialist dictatorship or government.

Currently, many leftist political parties in Western countries have become umbrella organizations to advocate exclusively for any number of minority groups that claim victimization. Consequently, the needs of the country's citizen majority are often disregarded, overlooked or disparaged because they are already the beneficiaries of so-called "white privilege.". This particular leftist doctrine is known as "identity politics."

36. The current obsession of many millennials with extreme political-correctness (PC)—of not offending any minority-group or causing any hurt feelings—has resulted in draconian measures of speech and thought control. For instance, any verbal, non-verbal or environmental communication that can be deemed as hurtful, offensive, derogatory or defamatory (whether intentional or not) by a minority-group member is termed a "microaggression."

As such, the leftist defenders of PC feel morally justified in responding to microaggressions with physical violence. Hypocritically, however, these same staunch "social justice warriors" (SJWs)—these same moralistic defenders of minority feelings—don't hesitate to toss openly-hostile microaggressions at majority-group members; such as Christians, or conservatives, or whites, or heterosexuals.

To further avoid the possibility that someone's feelings may be inadvertently hurt, offended, disturbed or traumatized, the self-appointed "PC police" expect that university lectures, internet sites, videos, movies, television shows and written articles include introductory alerts or "trigger warnings" about any emotionally-charged content. Critics contend that such efforts amount to infantilizing grown adults, and subtly eroding free speech.

But perhaps the ultimate in PC emotional protectionism is the recent creation of "safe spaces," particularly on university campuses. These are supposed areas where persons from various minority groups can gather and feel safe from discrimination, persecution, rejection and ridicule. Though well intentioned, safe spaces often devolve into echo chambers promoting group-think and speech censorship.

The pervasive emotional coddling and infantilizing among millennials in the name of political-correctness has led to them being described as "snowflakes," since their psychological and social overprotection often results in frenzied emotional breakdowns when confronted with the harsh reality of social events. The election of Donald Trump as US president in 2016, for example, caused a widespread hysteria that has been described as "Trump derangement syndrome" (TDS).

37. Even though certain liberal religious denominations (such as the Episcopal Church, the United Church of Christ and the United Church of Canada) will perform a same-sex religious ceremony, this does not transmute the union

into a sacramental marriage.

38. At the current level of medical intervention, a fetus born prior to 21 weeks of gestational development is estimated to have a 0% chance of survivability. However, by 26 weeks the fetus is estimated to have a 90% chance of survivability if born prematurely.

39. Every year in the US, there are about 1.3 million abortions. It is also estimated that somewhere between one and two million couples are waiting to adopt. Sadly, only 4% of women with unwanted pregnancies give their children up for adoption.

40. For deeper esoteric information on specific spirits of darkness, please refer to this authour's other publication: *From Darkness to Light: Divine Love and the Transmutation of Evil* (2016), available from Amazon.com.

SELECT BIBLIOGRAPHY

(in alphabetical order)

- *Catechism of the Catholic Church* (Our Sunday Visitor, Publishing Division, 2000)

- George Gamow, *One Two Three ... Infinity: Facts and Speculations of Science* (Bantam, 1972)

- Holy Bible, *RSV-CE* (Ignatius Press, 2006)

- Joel Bakan, *The Corporation: The Pathological Pursuit of Profit and Power* (Robinson Publishing, 2005)

- Lao-Tzu, *Tao Te Ching* (Wordsworth Editions, 1996)

- Magus Incognito, *The Secret Doctrine of the Rosicrucians* (Yogi Publication Society, 1949)

- Ron MacFarlane, *From Darkness to Light: Divine Love and the Transmutation of Evil* (Greater Mysteries Publications, 2016)

- Ron MacFarlane, *The Greater Mysteries of the Divine Trinity, the Logos-Word and Creation* (Greater Mysteries Publications, 2015)

- Rudolf Steiner, *Building Stones for an Understanding of the Mystery of Golgotha* (Rudolf Steiner Press, 1985)

- Rudolf Steiner, *Cosmic Memory: Prehistory of Earth and Man* (Harper & Row, 1981)

- Rudolf Steiner, *Foundations of Esotericism* (Rudolf Steiner Press, 1983)

- Rudolf Steiner, *Materialism and the Task of Anthroposophy* (SteinerBooks, 1987)

- Rudolf Steiner, *Supersensible Knowledge* (Anthroposophic Press, 1987)

- Rudolf Steiner, *The Fall of the Spirits of Darkness* (Rudolf Steiner Press, 1993)

- Rudolf Steiner, *The Influence of Spiritual Beings Upon Man* (Rudolf Steiner Press, 1982)

- Rudolf Steiner, *Theosophy of the Rosicrucian* (Rudolf Steiner Press, 1966)

- Three Initiates, *The Kybalion: A Study of the Hermetic Philosophy of Ancient Egypt and Greece* (Yogi Publication Society, 1940)

- Yogi Ramacharaka; *A Series of Lessons in Raja Yoga* (Yogi Publication Society, 1934)

OTHER BOOKS BY

RON MACFARLANE

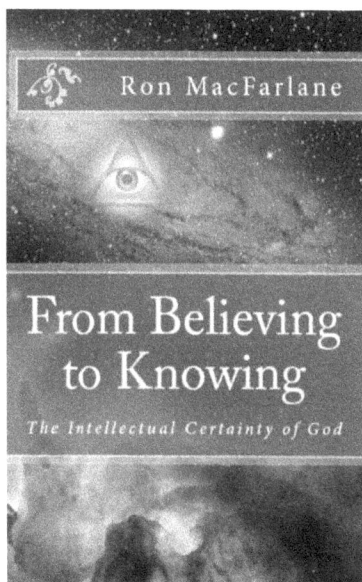

Ron MacFarlane

From Believing to Knowing

The Intellectual Certainty of God

THERE IS a puzzling and pervasive misconception in present-day thinking that the existence of God cannot be intellectually determined, and that mentally accepting the existence of God is strictly a matter of non-rational belief (faith).

As such, contemplating God's existence is erroneously regarded as the exclusive subject of faith-based or speculative ideologies (religion and philosophy) which have no proper place in natural scientific study.

The fact is, there are a number of very convincing intellectual arguments concerning the existence of God that have been around for hundreds of years. Indeed, the existence of God can be determined with compelling intellectual certainty—provided the thinker honestly wishes to do so. Moreover, recent advances and discoveries in science have not weakened previous intellectual arguments for God's existence, but instead have enormously strengthened and supported them.

Intellectually assenting to the existence of God is easily demonstrated to be a superlatively logical conclusion, not some vague irrational conceptualization. Remarkably, at the present time there are only two seriously-competing intellectual explanations of life: the existence of God (the "God-hypothesis") and the existence of infinite universes (the "multiverse theory"). The postulation of an infinite number of unobservable universes is clearly a desperate attempt by atheistic scientists to avoid the God-hypothesis as the most credible and logical intellectual explanation of life and the universe. Moreover, under intellectual scrutiny, the scientifically celebrated "evolutionary theory" is here demonstrated to be fatally-flawed (philosophically illogical) as a credible explanation of life.

In this particular discourse, five well-known intellectual arguments for God's existence will be thoroughly examined. In considering these arguments, every attempt has been made to include current contributions, advances and discoveries that have modernized the more traditional arguments. Prior to examining these particular arguments for God, the universal predilection to establish intellectual 'oneness'—"monism"—will be considered in detail as well as the recurring propensity to postulate the existence of one supreme being—"monotheism."

Once intellectual certainty of one Supreme Being is established, a number of divine attributes can be logically deduced as well. Eleven of these attributes will be determined and examined in greater detail.

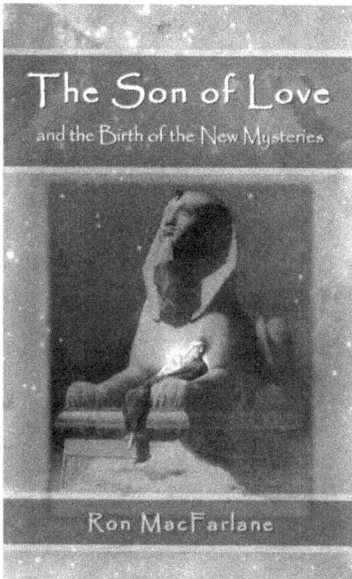

The Son of Love
and the Birth of the New Mysteries

Ron MacFarlane

FOR COUNTLESS esoteric students today, the Mystery centres of ancient times have retained a powerful and fascinating allure. Moreover, there is often a wishful longing to revive and continue their secretive initiatory activity into modern times.

Unfortunately, this anachronistic longing is largely based on an illusionary misunderstanding of these Mysteries and the real reasons for their destined demise.

The primary reason for the disappearance of the ancient Mysteries is that they have been supplanted by the superior new mysteries—the mysteries of the Son. These new mysteries were initiated by Christ-Jesus himself. In order to better understand these Son-mysteries in a spiritually-scientific way, Rudolf Steiner (1861–1925) established the Anthroposophical Movement and Society.

Unfortunately, anthroposophy today has become unduly influenced by members and leaders who long to transform spiritual science into a modern-day Mystery institution. Moreover, contrary to his own words and intentions, Rudolf Steiner is even claimed to be the founder of some new "Michael-Mysteries."

By carefully establishing a correct esoteric understanding of the ancient pagan Mysteries, as well as a better appreciation of the new mysteries of the Son, this well-researched and readable discourse convincingly shows that all current and past attempts to revive the ancient pagan Mysteries regressively diverts human development backward to the seducer of mankind, Lucifer, rather than progressively forward to the saviour of mankind, Christ-Jesus.

Moreover, by additionally tracing the intriguing historical development of esoteric Christianity (particularly the Knights of the Holy Grail and Rosicrucianism) alongside Freemasonry, the Knights Templar and Theosophy, this important and necessary study illuminates the correct esoteric position and true significance of anthroposophical spiritual science.

This book is available to order from Amazon.com

Physical Science to Spiritual Science

The Future Development of Intellectual Thought

Ron MacFarlane

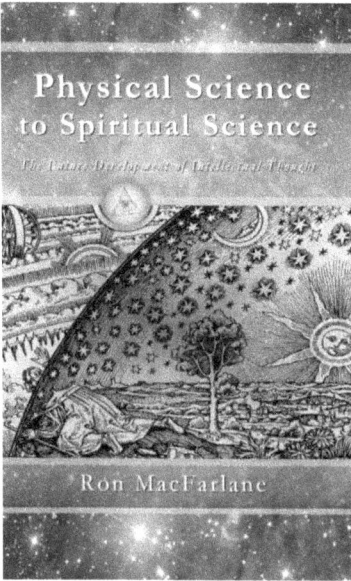

THE PRIDE OF civilized mankind—intellectual thinking—is at a critical crossroads today. No doubt surprising to many, the cognitive capacity to consciously formulate abstract ideas in the mind, and then to manipulate them according to devised rules of logic in order to acquire new knowledge has only been humanly possible for about the last 3,000 years. Prior to intellectual (abstract) thinking, mental activity characteristically consisted of vivid pictorial images that arose spontaneously in the human mind from natural and supernatural stimuli.

The ability to think abstractly is the necessary foundation for mathematics, language and empirical science. The developmental history of intellectual thought, then, exactly parallels the developmental history of mathematics, language and science. Moreover, since abstract thinking inherently encourages the cognitive separation of subject (the thinker) and object (the perceived environment), the history of intellectual development also parallels the historical development of self-conscious (ego) awareness.

Over the last 3000 years, mankind in general has slowly perfected intellectual thinking; and thereby developed complex mathematics, sophisticated languages, comprehensively-detailed empirical sciences and pronounced ego-awareness. Unfortunately, all this intellectual activity over the many previous centuries has also exclusively strengthened human awareness of the physical, material world and substantially decreased awareness of the superphysical spiritual world.

That is why today, intellectual thinking is at a critical crossroads in further development. Thinking (intellectual or otherwise) is a superphysical activity—an activity within the soul. Empirical science is incorrect in postulating that physical brain tissue generates thought. The brain is simply the biological "sending and receiving" apparatus: sending sense-perceptions to the soul and receiving thought-conceptions from the soul. All this activity certainly generates chemical and electrical activity within the brain; but this activity is the effect, not the cause of thinking.

The danger to future intellectual thought is that increased acceptance of the erroneous scientific notion that thinking is simply brain-chemistry will increasingly deny and deaden true superphysical thinking. Future thinking runs the risk of becoming "a self-fulfilled prophecy"—the more people fervently believe that thought is simply brain-chemistry, the more thought will indeed become simply brain-chemistry. As a result, future human beings will be less responsible for generating their own thinking activity and more involuntarily controlled by their own brain chemistry. The artificial intelligence of machines won't become more human; but instead human beings will become more like robotic machines.

Presently, then, empirical science is leading intellectual thinking in a downward, materialistic direction. Correspondingly, however, true spiritual science (anthroposophy) is also actively engaged in leading intellectual thought back to its superphysical source in the soul. *Physical Science to Spiritual Science: the Future Development of Intellectual Thought* begins by examining the historical development of intellectual thinking and the corresponding rise of physical science. Once this has been discussed, practical and detailed information is presented on how spiritual science is leading intellectual thinking back to its true soul-source. It is intended that upon completion of this discourse, sincere and open-minded readers will themselves come to experience the exhilarating, superphysical nature of their own intellectual thought.

THE DIVINE TRINITY—the greatest of all Christian mysteries. How is it that the one God is a unity of three divine persons? Christ-Jesus first revealed this mystery to his disciples when on earth. Later, around the sixth century, the Trinitarian mystery was theologically clarified and outlined by the formulation of the Athanasian Creed. Conceptual understanding of the divine Trinity has changed very little in Western society since then. Similarly with the theological understanding of the Logos-Word, as mentioned in the Gospel of St. John. The traditional understanding, that has remained essentially unchallenged for centuries, is that the Logos-Word is synonymous with God the Son. As for creation, the best that mainstream Christianity has historically provided is an ancient, allegorical account contained in the Book of Genesis.

Out of the hidden well-springs of esoteric Christianity, and as the title indicates, *The Greater Mysteries of the Divine Trinity, the Logos-Word and Creation*, delves much more deeply into the profound mysteries of the Trinitarian God, the Logos-Word of St. John and the creation of the universe. The divine Trinity is here demonstrated to be the loving union of Heavenly Father, Holy Mother and Eternal Son. The Logos-Word is here evidenced to be the "Universal Man," the primordial cosmic creation of God the Son. Universal creation itself is here detailed to be the "one life becoming many"—the multiplication of the Logos-Word into countless individualized life forms and beings.

The depth and breadth of original and thought-provoking information presented here will, no doubt, stimulate and excite those esoteric thinkers who are seriously seeking answers to the deeper mysteries of life, existence and the universe.

This book is available to order from Amazon.com

Ron MacFarlane

The Star of Higher
Knowledge

The Five Guiding Mysteries of
Esoteric Christianity

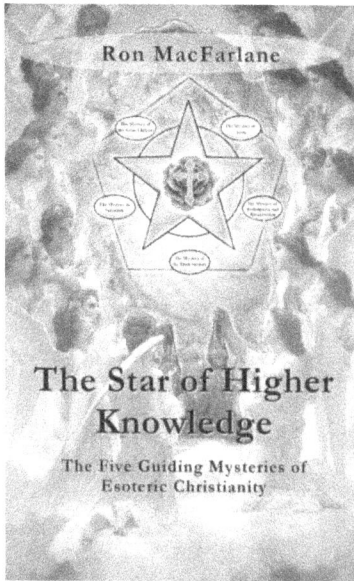

WHEN CHRIST-JESUS walked the earth over two thousand years ago, he established a two-fold division in his teaching that has continued to this day. To the general public, he simplified his teaching and presented it in pictorial, allegorical and figurative imagery in the form of stories, parables and lessons that could be imaginatively and intuitively understood.

To his inner circle of disciples (who were sufficiently prepared), however, he taught intellectual concepts, clear ideas and logical reasoning that could be understood on a much deeper and wider level of comprehension. As biblically explained:

> Then the disciples came and said to him, "Why do you speak to them [the general public] in parables?" And he answered them, "To you it has been given to know the secrets of the kingdom of heaven, but to them it has not been given ... This is why I speak to them in parables, because seeing they do not see, and hearing they do not hear, nor do they understand." (Matt 13:10, 13)

Moreover, in union with the divine, Our Saviour was able to reveal sacred knowledge that had never been previously presented in the entire history of mankind: "I will explain mysteries hidden since the creation of the world" (Matt 13:35). This sacred and revealed knowledge has been termed "Christ-mysteries" or "mysteries of the Son."

After his glorious resurrection and ascension, Christ-Jesus

institutionalized his two-fold mystery-teachings through St. Peter and St. John (the evangelist, not the apostle). Through St. Peter, Our Saviour instituted a universal Christian *religion* and *theology* to preserve, promote and convey the more basic and simplified mystery-teachings that are intended for the general public. Through St. John, Christ-Jesus instituted a universal Christian *philosophy* and *theosophy* to preserve, promote and convey the more comprehensive and complex mystery-teachings that are intended for the more advanced disciples (Christian initiates). In esoteric terminology, the institutionalized teachings through St. Peter are known as the "lesser mysteries of exoteric Christianity." The institutionalized teachings through St. John are known as the "greater mysteries of esoteric Christianity."

While both mystery-teaching approaches are equally sacred, profound and intended to complement each other, corrupt and intolerant authorities within the universal institution (Church) of St. Peter, for many centuries, persecuted and attacked any public expressions of esoteric Christianity. Consequently, genuine historical forms of esoteric Christianity, such as the Knights of the Holy Grail and the Fraternity of the Rose-Cross, were forced to be secretive and publically-hidden during the past two thousand years.

Thankfully today, the social, political and intellectual climate has progressed to the point where the greater mystery-teachings of esoteric Christianity can begin to be publically revealed for the first time. This modern-day outpouring really began with the twentieth-century establishment of anthroposophy by Rudolf Steiner (1861–1925). The information and approach presented in *The Star of Higher Knowledge: The Five Guiding Mysteries of Esoteric Christianity* is intended to augment and continue the mystery-teachings of Christ-Jesus as safeguarded by the Rosicrucian Fraternity and publicized through anthroposophy.

Consequently, this particular discourse delves much more deeply and comprehensively into the cosmos-changing salvational achievement of Christ-Jesus: the historical and cosmic preparations; as well as his birth, life, death, resurrection and ascension. While much of this mystery information may be unfamiliar, unknown and unexpected to mainstream (exoteric) Christianity, it in no way is meant to criticize, denigrate or displace the profound teachings of the universal Church; but rather, to complement, to enhance and to enlarge—for the betterment of true Christianity and, thereby, the betterment of all mankind.

This book is available to order from Amazon.com

Also check out the authour's website:

www.heartofshambhala.com

A Site Dedicated to True Esoteric Christianity

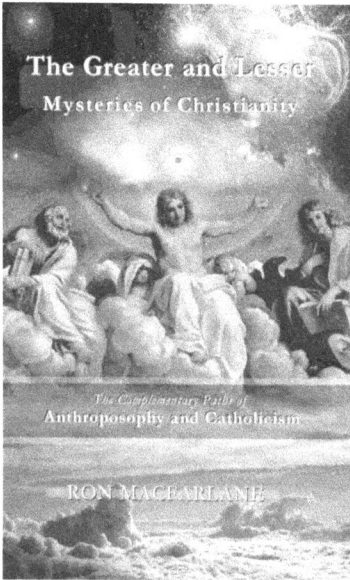

Contemporary Christianity, the world religion established by the God-Man, Christ-Jesus, and founded on the revelatory-principle that "God is love," is hardly the shining example of ideological unity and universal brotherhood that it was intended to be. There are approximately 41,000 different Christian denominations in the world today, many of which are fervently hostile to each other.

Atheistic and anti-Christian polemicists have concluded that there is something inherently wrong with Christianity itself and, in consequence, it is doomed to failure and eventual extinction.

Discerning Christian advocates, however, know that any apparent failure to realize the high ideals of Christianity is not due to the profound teachings and the illustrious life-example of Christ-Jesus, but instead to the limitations of wounded human nature. Corrupt, power-hungry, destructive and evil-minded human beings have twisted, distorted and fragmented true Christianity for the past two thousand years, and continue to do so today.

Moreover, on a much deeper spiritual level, since Christianity is indeed a divinely-initiated endeavor to help restore "fallen" humanity, powerful and demonic beings have attempted to destroy nascent Christianity from its very inception. But thankfully, according to Christ-Jesus himself, "the powers of hell will not prevail against it [Christianity]" (Matt 16:18).

Sadly contributing to the injurious fragmentation of Christianity—the "religion of divine love"—is the sectarian hostility between certain proponents of anthroposophy and select members of the Catholic Church. In both cases, this is largely due to ignorance; that is, an almost complete lack of understanding about the true significance and mission of the other—anthroposophical critics know almost nothing of Catholicism, and Catholic critics know almost nothing about anthroposophy.

The wonderful reconciliatory fact is that anthroposophy and Catholicism are not conflicting polar opposites, but are instead like two sides of the same golden coin—different, but complementary. Instead of only one side or the other being the only true approach to Christ-Jesus, both are uniquely necessary and both positively contribute to the complete truth of Christianity.

Since this author is happily and harmoniously both an anthroposophist and a Catholic, *The Greater and Lesser Mysteries of Christianity: The Complementary Paths of Anthroposophy and Catholicism* earnestly seeks to correct the misinformation and lack of understanding that each partisan critic has for the other. As in almost every significant dispute, increased knowledge and familiarity about each other will in time bring both sides closer together for mutual growth and benefit.

This book is available to order from Amazon.com

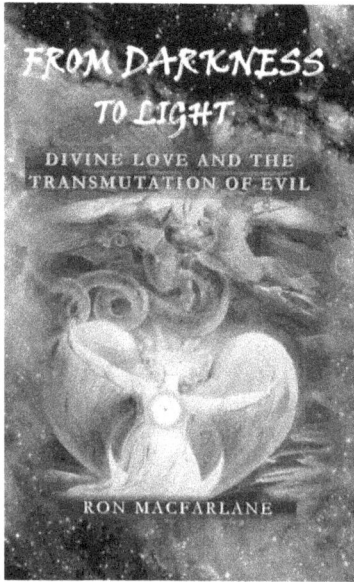

IN THE LIGHT of spiritual science, never before in the history of the world has there been such an assailment of supernatural evil upon humanity as extensive and intense as there exists at the present time. Subconsciously pouring into the human soul are the seductive whisperings of Luciferic beings and fallen angels; the perceptual distortions of Ahrimanic (Satanic) beings; the lurid, egocentric promptings of corrupt spirits of personality (asuras); and the violent inducements of blood-lust rising up from the subterranean "beast of Revelation" (Sorath the sun-demon).

The tragic and bitter irony of all this, however, is that because of today's pervasive, atheistic and secular culture and the materialistic worldview of natural science, individual human beings are correspondingly the most oblivious to supernatural evil than they have ever been at any other time in world history.

To be sure, people today are certainly aware of the *effects* of supernatural evil—extensive and increased natural disasters; horrific instances of mass genocide; the prolific use of torture and brutality by government agencies; individual acts of sudden cruelty and murder; pathological selfishness throughout the world's business and financial markets; strange, globally-infectious viral contagions; the devaluation of human life through abortion and euthanasia; and a world-wide pandemic of dehumanizing drug addiction. What most people today fail to realize is that the invisible fomenting agents—the *causes*—of all these life-threatening, destructive physical events and pathologies are ultimately rooted in the impulses of supernatural evil.

To be sure, mankind would have completely and totally succumbed to this tsunami of supernatural evil if it weren't for the protective and opposing intervention of powerful, benevolent celestial beings, such as St. Michael the Archai, Yahweh-Elohim (the spirit of the moon), and the Solar-Christos (aka: "Christ"—the regent of the sun).

More than ever, it is crucially important in today's world to understand the nature of evil, and to become more aware and cognizant of the various perpetrators of supernatural evil. Thereby, conscious cooperation with the compassionate protectors and guardians of mankind can be increased and strengthened, so that supernatural evil is better resisted and eventually overcome.

To this end, *From Darkness to Light: Divine Love and the Transmutation of Evil* delves deeply into the thorny questions of "What exactly is evil?", together with "How and when did evil begin?", as well as "Why does God allow evil to exist?" Once the nature, genesis and purpose of evil is better understood, then various influential superphysical perpetrators of supernatural evil will be examined in closer detail. Correspondingly, the superphysical proponents of cosmic holiness will be identified and better understood as well.

Wherever possible, the spiritual-scientific research of anthroposophy—an independent offshoot of the Rosicrucian Fraternity, and the modern-day expression of esoteric Christianity that was established by Rudolf Steiner (1861–1925)—will be included and referenced. Following this profoundly-esoteric background, the destined human struggle with continuing and obdurate evil—far into the future development of the earth—will also be mentally envisioned and supersensibly examined.

It is sincerely intended that upon completion of the entire written discourse, concerned individuals will be better armed and shielded in order to become actively engaged on the side of holiness and spiritual light in the prolonged cosmic battle against evil and material darkness.

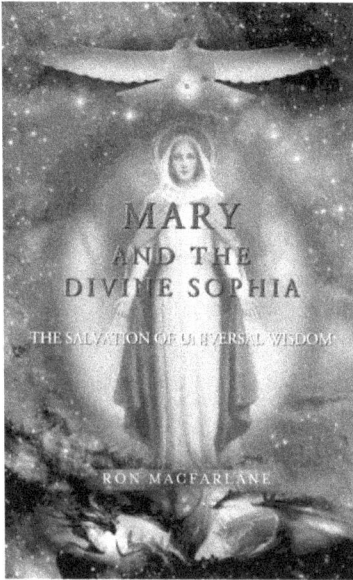

NO DOUBT, anyone interested in Christian esotericism will have noticed that there is a widespread modern-day revival of interest in the ancient gnostic concept of "Sophia" amongst a strange diversity of groups: wiccans, neo-pagans, New Agers, neo-gnostics, Catholic mystics, Orthodox Christians, radical feminists and anthropos-ophists. Adding to this ideological mélange is the exotic variety of Sophia designations and conceptions: the Divine Sophia, the heavenly-sophia, the earthly-sophia, Hagia Sophia, the goddess Sophia, the Aeon Sophia, the Virgin Sophia, Sophia-Achamoth, Pistis Sophia, Isis-Sophia, Jesus Sophia, theo-sophia, philo-sophia and anthropo-sophia.

Not surprisingly, then, this cacophony of Sophias is very often contradictory, confusing, distorted, invented, erroneous, and (sadly) rarely enlightening. It is not difficult to detect that "esoteric entrepreneurs" have seized this current "thirst for Sophia" to offer up a potpourri of books, courses, conferences, workshops, lessons, websites, video clips, internet articles—even worship services—to inundate, titillate and financially captivate any novice Sophia seeker.

So, what is a sincere Christian esotericist to make of this fervent Sophia phenomenon: "Is it a positive and healthy spiritual development, or is it a regressive and outmoded religious diversion?" This particular discourse—*Mary and the Divine Sophia*—delves deeply and genuinely into this important question in order to establish spiritual fact from unspiritual fiction.

In order to adequately answer this question, however, profound esoteric investigation into the Trinitarian nature of God, as well as the universal being of the Logos-Word, together with the fundamental underlying principles of the created cosmos will need to be detailed and discussed. Some of this previously-guarded esoteric information may be quite new and unfamiliar to many readers; but every effort has been made to present it in clear, understandable concepts.

Furthermore, since the mother of Jesus is very often intimately associated or connected to historical and present-day conceptions of Sophia, a comprehensive study will also be undertaken regarding Mary and her special relationship to the Divine Sophia; relying heavily on the spiritual-scientific research of Austrian philosopher and esotericist, Rudolf Steiner (1861–1925). Once again, a great deal of this information will be startlingly new to those unfamiliar with anthroposophy; but, as before, great care has been taken to present this possibly-unfamiliar information in a comprehensible, intellectually-accessible way.

It is sincerely intended that this discourse will provide the earnest esotericist with reliable, trustworthy and objective spiritual knowledge in order to confidently know and understand the mystery-truth of the heavenly-sophia; and thereby extricate her from the distortions and falsifications of Lucifer and Ahriman.

This book is available to order from Amazon.com